ENTS

URE,

SIGN

LUCY
BULLIVANT

V&A
CONTEMPORARY

First published by V&A
Publications, 2006

V&A Publications
Victoria and Albert Museum
South Kensington
London SW7 2RL

Distributed in North America
by Harry N. Abrams, Inc.,
New York

ISBN 10 1851774815
ISBN-13 9781851774814
Library of Congress Control
Number 2006924189

10 9 8 7 6 5 4 3 2 1
2010 2009 2008 2007 2006

V&A Publications
Victoria and Albert Museum
South Kensington
London SW7 2RL
www.vam.ac.uk

Designed by
Graphic Thought Facility

Cover illustration:
Body Movies:
Relational Architecture
Projection
Rafael Lozano-Hemmer
Schouwburgplein, Rotterdam,
The Netherlands
see p.36

Printed in China

RESPONSIVE ENVIRONMENTS

ACKNOWLEDGEMENTS

I would like to thank all the architects, designers, artists and other creative practitioners featured in this book wholeheartedly for their high-level stimulation, time and visual material, especially Usman Haque and Tobi Schneidler for suggestions and expert comments; Hannah Redler, Curator of Art Programmes at the Science Museum, London, for dialogues on interactivity and museological practice; Ole Bouman, editor of 'Volume', for an inestimably valued professional collaboration since 1996; David Turnbull, Antonino Saggio, Vicente Guallart, Stefano Mirti, Walter Aprile, Mike Weinstock, Marco Brizzi and Robert Violette for their insights and enthusiasm; John Thackara for hospitality at his international Doors of Perception conferences, especially 'Flow', 2003, enabling investigation at closer range; Tony Dunne and Fiona Raby for inspiring conversations over eighteen years; Helen Castle, editor, 'AD', Shane Walter and Anna Doyle, onedotzero, and Vivienne Guskin at the ICA, London, for their collaboration on the 4dspace projects; V2 Institute for Unstable Media, Rotterdam, for creative input, and Peter Murray and Stella Buchan-Ioannou of the London Architecture Biennale 2006 for taking on board Carol Brown and Mette Ramsgaard Thomsen's latest interactive dance production. Appreciative thanks to Jane Pavitt, University of Brighton Senior Research Fellow in Product Design at the V&A Museum, for commissioning me to write this book; Graphic Thought Facility for their considered design of it; Mary Butler and Monica Woods of V&A Publications for expertly overseeing the book's production, and Krystyna Mayer for editing the text. For perpetual encouragement, thanks are due to Dargan, Pat, Helena, Alex and Victoria Bullivant and to friends indeed Dan Knight, Shona Kitchen, Christine Styrnau, Torsten Neeland, Fiona Dunlop and Tobias Kommerell.

AUTHOR BIOGRAPHY

Lucy Bullivant is an architectural critic, author and curator of exhibitions and conferences. She has written regularly about architecture, urban and 3D design since 1987, and contributes to 'Domus', 'The Plan', 'Volume', 'a+u', 'Indesign', 'Harvard Design Magazine', 'The Architect's Newspaper', 'Blueprint' and 'The Sunday Review' ('Independent on Sunday'). Her major international touring exhibitions include Kid size: the material world of childhood (Vitra Design Museum, 1997–2005), Space Invaders: new UK architecture (British Council, with Pedro Gadanho, 2001–3) and The near and the far, fixed and in flux (XIX Milan Triennale, 1996). She has curated several international conferences, including 4dspace: interactive architecture (ICA, 2003, and AA, 2005), Spaced Out III (ICA, 1997) and Shared Territories (RCA, 2006), and is the author of 'Anglo Files: UK architecture's rising generation' (Thames & Hudson, 2005) and guest editor of 4dspace: interactive architecture (Wiley Academy/AD, 2005). She regularly chairs events and lectures internationally.

INTRODUCTION

RESPONSIVE ENVIRONMENTS – BY DEFINITION SPACES THAT INTERACT WITH THE PEOPLE WHO USE THEM, PASS THROUGH THEM OR BY THEM – HAVE IN A VERY SHORT SPACE OF TIME BECOME UBIQUITOUS.

Responsive environments – by definition spaces that interact with the people who use them, pass through them or by them – have in a very short space of time become ubiquitous. Not just confined to the fantasy worlds of films like 'Minority Report', 'ExistenZ' or 'The Matrix', digital technology-enabled spaces, notoriously employing unprecedented levels of CCTV as well as demonstrating the seemingly infinite powers of multimedia, have invaded our lives, fundamentally affecting the identity of public, corporate, retail and cultural spaces, and connecting remote environments. The widespread impact of personal digital technology has reached the point where both Britain's queen and the president of the United States own iPods.[1] Nearly two-thirds of the UK's population has Internet access at home, and the same percentage has digital television. Electronic billboards have been around for decades, but now the concept of connectivity has also literally seeped into the skins of buildings in new ways. Artists are responding to the electro-physical flux of urban environments, co-opting responsive dynamic media systems, wireless sensing, wearable computing and even topological media. They proactively consult scientific institutions to dig deeper into their topics, and are not interested in 'tech' or smart spaces for the sake of it, but to create environments that act as mediating devices for a new social statement.

While IT applied purely commercially for applications and products always focuses on new technologies' speed and efficiency, the respon-sive projects featured in this book – many of them using customized low-tech elements – engage through experiment with our wishes and bodily sensations on an existential level. Their impact is phenomenolog-ical, meaning that the body is able to directly experience its environment in a very direct and personal way. A number of young architects have chosen to create interactive spaces instead of designing and constructing buildings in the more traditional sense. Their interests now overlap strongly with those of designers and artists. All these professions now work with new technologies. Many, moreover, through trial and error, are becoming 'humanist technologists', as artist and professor at MIT John Maeda has called designers striving to make technology not just easier to use, but also more closely connected to our bodies and senses.[2] Most are far more concerned with the quality of human interaction technology makes possible than with the human-computer interface (HCI), but that relationship has to be intuitively designed and then exhaustively prototyped to achieve credible results. This shift in priorities transcends objects, to reinvent design as more of an event-based installation concept – an approach that is of huge value now that the best visitor attractions, museums and galleries are striving to open up to more participatory ways of engaging their publics.

THE PUBLIC
Early concept designs for gallery spaces
with 'trees' carrying input devices off
the trunks and content in their foliage.
West Bromwich, UK
Ben Kelly Design
(architect: Alsop Architects;
visitor interfaces: AllofUs)
2004–5, see p.105

Its success also hinges on effective new forms of collaboration between disciplines. A responsive environment is the result of creative work by artists, architects, designers and other specialists needed to help realize it – not just software engineers and/or robotics specialists, but frequently also scientists. Rather than being wholly computer generated, like virtual reality projects, responsive environments are a bridge between the physical and the virtual. Historically, such works have been the domain of media artists. However, architects have long since evolved their aspirations through the use of digital techniques and technologies and sensors to bring architecture literally closer to media by transforming it into a real-time medium. This has been one way to compensate for the marginalization of architecture as a cultural activity. Meanwhile new media designers have become genuinely more spatial in their approach to projects. Digital technologies are fostering an experimental dissolution of disciplinary forms; working with space is no longer the exclusive preserve of architects, and architects no longer confine themselves to traditional visual devices and sources of inspiration.

In the 1980s and '90s a good deal of cutting-edge architecture relied upon theory alone. Now it ironically risks becoming a screen-based medium in its adherence to imagery, with drawbacks as well as advantages. Art, meanwhile, has long since embraced the idea of the event. The very nature of responsive environments, involving functioning through interfaces that facilitate interaction, is a form of mediation between the inner world of the self and the outside world, and it presupposes some kind of event that is not wholly pre-programmed. Input from the real world received via sensors is essential, as are output devices in the form of actuators (mechanisms that transform an electrical input signal into motion[3]), displays or other sensory phenomena to engage with users. That engagement is multi-modal across all the senses. The question is, what happens next?

'Architects who wish to pursue an advanced conceptual agenda often create work that treads a fine line between art and architecture,' says Usman Haque (born Washington DC, USA, 1971), an architect who creates responsive environments. To do this they use some of the techniques and tactics developed by new media artists, but sometimes they go further than the interactive work devised by artists, creating circular systems, as Haque has defined it, that embrace cybernetics and are usually based on customized technology tools. Not only content to see how an observer fits into the scenario, these works explore how the output of the observer/participant maps on to the relationship between the input and the output.

ARCHITECTS WHO WISH TO PURSUE AN ADVANCED CONCEPTUAL AGENDA OFTEN CREATE WORK THAT TREADS A FINE LINE BETWEEN ART AND ARCHITECTURE.

USMAN HAQUE

FRESH WATER PAVILION
Lars Spuybroek/NOX
Installation for the H2O EXPO Neeltje Jans
near Rotterdam, the Netherlands
1997

Interactive media is often misunderstood as something that is only part of audio visual devices like DVD players or multimedia software, but our grasp of its potential is extending into an awareness of how it engages with other realms of the senses and at a real-life human scale. The service design experience has become important, and the new thinking of designers is flooding the mainstream. The best services keep things very simple, like the iPod, a mobile resource for playing music, simultaneously connecting the wearer with an online, virtual music store. Evolving effective responsive systems, and creating a credible interface between the work and the user, requires an awareness of many different types of user, contexts and function, as well as the phenomenonological aspects of social and environmental conditions.

Traditionally, architecture has been about hardware, about form and enclosure by means of floors, walls and a roof. Designers such as Dunne + Raby (Tony Dunne, born London, 1964 and Fiona Raby, born Singapore, 1963), whose 'FLIRT'[4] used mobile telephones and software programs to investigate the relationship between digital communication and how people experience their environments, have radically departed from the traditional architectural notions of space. This book also focuses on the relationship between the physical and the digital, an 'in-between' space. Architecture sets its own programmatic agenda, without becoming art, and becomes intelligent, cybernetic, like natural artefacts that are themselves able to evolve and adapt to their environment, their inhabitants and other sensory stimuli. Pioneering buildings like Lars Spuybroek's **'FRESH WATER PAVILION'** [5] and Kas Oosterhuis's 'Salt Water Pavilion' for the H2O EXPO (built in Neeltje Jans near Rotterdam in 1997) – both multimedia exhibitions of water – are ludic, yet hermetic environments, driven by desire and subjectivity, organisms so synthetic that they close the distinction between the artificial and the natural.

Other architects engage interactive designers to help achieve their effects, as in the case of Diller & Scofidio,[6] who asked Steve Rubin of EAR Studio to make the interactive elements of '**BLUR**', their installation in Switzerland in 2002.[7] Many other prototypes have been made, especially in academia, for instance by the Architectural Association's Design Research Laboratory (DRL),[8] involving research into the ways that architectural space – including building materials and the sensors and controls guiding their performance – already operate as live, dynamic fields of force, movement and flow. The buildings affect the actions of those present and vice versa, and architecture's traditional sense of social responsibility, filtered through the notion of play, is reinvented as a more 'modal' way of using space, an ever-changing modality.

In order to get to that point, the software systems designed to create the interfaces in the first place are in themselves rendered almost alive, with their own personalities. As Sherry Turkle has pointed out,[9] 'windows' and 'links' have become potent metaphors for a multiplicity of perspectives and for the expression of different aspects of self – and place. If architects want to create a responsive environment, they need to think like designers of operating systems. A system or framework is still needed, but it is subordinate to the means of expression provided by the software.

The expectations placed on responsive environments as a field have changed immensely. The groundbreaking exhibition Cybernetic Serendipity, curated by Jasia Reichardt and staged at the ICA in 1968, featured a host of cybernetic environments, sculptures and remote-control robots alongside computer-generated graphics, computer-animated films, computer-composed and played music and presented verse. As Reichardt recalls in 2004, 'at the time computers had not revolutionized music, or art, or poetry, in the same way they had revolutionized science… with the advent of computers the world of art expanded beyond its conventional boundaries'.[10] Even without it, artists such as James Turrell and Krzysztof Wodiczko were imagining new functions for urban objects and spaces. Reichardt observed the waning of interest in cybernetic art in Britain in the 1970s and '80s, while in the 1980s Japan became more interested in technological art and emotional design.[11]

MEMORY WALL
Interactive wall
Jason Bruges
Architect of foyer and bedroom suites:
Kathryn Findlay
Hotel Puerta América, Madrid, Spain
Commissioned by Grupo Urvasco
2005

This culminated in 1997, when the Nippon Telegraph and Telephone Corporation (NTT) established the Intercommunication Center (ICC) in Tokyo Opera City Tower. NTT was a new form of museum 'interfacing scientific and artistic cultures in the electronic information age'.[12] Austria's Ars Electronica, a festival for art, technology and science, and museum of digital and media art in Linz, came into being as early as 1979. It has now begun to explore its own history of media art with international exhibitions in Asia.[13] Germany launched the ZKM,[14] which carries out production and research and stages exhibitions and events, in Karlsruhe in the same year, and the V2 Institute for the Unstable Media was launched in 1981. Its very name reflected its aim to present a view of the world that was 'complex and variable', rather than 'orderly and consistent'.[15]

Nowadays BAFTA (the British Academy of Film and Television Arts) has its own Interactive Design Award, and in 2005 Ars Electronica presented the first ever international conference on the histories of media art, science and technology, on location at the Banff Centre in Canada, frequently host to media art events. San José's 2006 hosting of ISEA's biannual International Symposium of Electronic Art, first held in Utrecht in the Netherlands in 1988, down the road from California's Silicon Valley, brings together the international art, architecture, design, science and technology communities.[16] The extent of the cross-fertilization of ideas that now goes on due to the nomadic nature of these institutions is also more than matched by the 'global' activities of spatial interactive design practitioners. Characterized by looser groupings than those of the institutions, their impact is sporadic yet no less dynamic.

IF INTELLIGENT SPACES WERE TRULY INTELLIGENT, WE MIGHT NOT LIKE THEM, BECAUSE WE WANT THEM TO BE INTELLIGENT BUT ACQUIESCENT.

LO–REZ–DOLORES–TABULA–RASA
Installation with fibre optics pixels
embedded in Corian™
Ron Arad
Installation film: The Light Surgeons
Producer: Gallery Mourmans
Exhibited at the 9th Venice Architecture
Biennale, Italy 2004

The technologies involved, of sensing, computation and display, are in rapid flux, so anachronistic solutions need to be avoided and a prototype-based approach is essential. Platforms need to be robust; breakdowns are an occupational and institutional hazard, and new schemes are not foolproof, as illustrated by the recent UK discussion about whether an intrusive network of biometric readers[17] is necessary for the government's new ID card scheme to work. Commercial digital products are multi-functional – for instance the mobile phone converged with the camera and tape recorder; similarly, designers are extending the versatility of equipment for crafted responsive environments to enable different sensing modalities. The difference is that they customize what exists in order to achieve the right results. Usman Haque feels that 'new media artists and architects do not necessarily need the precision and accuracy that scientists do in order to explore the poetries of interaction'. They often do not require very sophisticated equipment to develop truly interesting interactive projects, using artefacts to hand, and are comfortable with the idea of 'hacking' existing technology to make customized interfaces, sensors, biofeedback devices and actuators employing relatively simple technology.

MUSCLE TRANS-PORTS
Pavilion prototype
ONL/Kas Oosterhuis
Installation at the Venice Architecture
Biennale, Italy, 2002;
included in the exhibition Non-Standard
Architecture, Pompidou Centre, Paris, France
2003

THE TECHNOLOGIES INVOLVED, OF SENSING, COMPUTATION AND DISPLAY, ARE IN RAPID FLUX, SO ANACHRONISTIC SOLUTIONS NEED TO BE AVOIDED AND A PROTOTYPE-BASED APPROACH IS ESSENTIAL.

Haque, together with Adam Somlai-Fischer (born Budapest, Hungary, 1976) of aether architecture, designed a kit of parts – sensors and actuators – from hacked toys such as inexpensive kid's walkie-talkies and desk fans, as well as other devices that artists and architects could use. When they want to experiment with responsive system concepts, particularly on large, urban-scale projects, Haque feels that the complexity, logistics or sheer costs prevent their prototype research unless a suitable investor or sponsor can be found. A solution lies with what he calls 'open-source architecture', combining reusability and low tech.[18] Putting this in a global, industrialized context, experimental design of this kind is made under conditions where production possibilities are changing all the time, and desktop digital media is affordable; in the developing world, reusability and low tech are a necessity.

The merging of architectural and artistic skills to make responsive environments has resulted in the blurring of professional boundaries. This is allowing work to be created that explores questions about the various legacies of modernity – climatic homogeneity, CCTV and a whole range of potential communications – through bodily relationships between humans mediated by technology that would otherwise not be tapped into. Participative works represent ongoing research into the architecture of non-visual environments, using sound, smell, and electromagnetic and thermal phenomena, and strive to go beyond what we already think we know. This work builds on the pioneering design researches of the 1970s into 'design primario',[19] focusing on the user's direct physical perception rather than semiotics of form, and the interest in 'info-eco' ideas of John Thackara, Ezio Manzini and Marco Susani.[20]

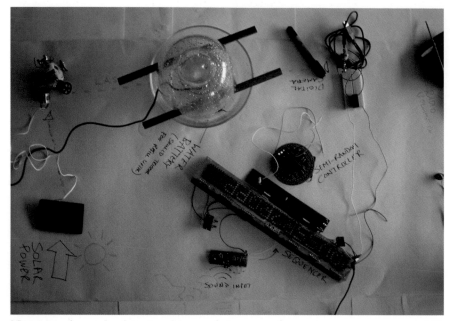

LOW-TECH SENSORS AND ACTUATORS
Prototypes
Haque Design+Research and aether
architecture (Adam Somlai-Fischer)
Commissioned by the Foundation for Art and
Creative Technology (FACT), Liverpool, UK
2004—5

Not just about the haptic, this work is part of a major, more recent shift in design in the industrialized world towards experience design,[21] a conceptual approach that aims to create an emotional relationship with individuals, connecting at the level of perception of personal value.[22] It shifts the emphasis from the machine to its intelligence and its distribution through an environment of 'intelligent ambience',[23] and is based on an understanding of people's character, behaviour and context. In the best instances, through a direct, unmediated relationship with a person, the trait of a product enables it to be perceived in a phenomeno-logically satisfying way. This implies entering the 'real world' of people's bodily experience. Emotional design is one means by which design can differentiate itself in a globalized world with an over-accumulation of branded products that deny cultural difference. Phenomenological design applied commercially (for RFID tags, for instance) risks coercion or monitoring; in a speculative art-based context, it opens new possibi-lities for experiences.

While in the public educational context of museums and visitor attrac-tions, as well as in corporate environments such as Bloomberg's head-quarters, designers and artists contracted for specific projects need to identify the best ways to dovetail and communicate concepts, artefacts, data and experiences. Artists and designers working to self-briefs (for speculative installations that may find their way into a range of contexts) use technology more speculatively. Technology is deployed as a means of understanding and commenting on paradoxes within our culture, especially the unquestioned ubiquity of corporate technologies, as well as to make visible or to translate invisible phenomena ranging from sounds to pollution, electromagnetic waves and the paranormal. Human desires are a fundamental part of this list. Mexican media artist Rafael Lozano-Hemmer (born Mexico, 1967) believes that art needs to avoid what art critic Lorne Falk has called 'technological correctness'[24] – works that merely parade their novel qualities and special effects – in favour of those embracing intervention, process, criticism and humour.

If intelligent spaces were truly intelligent, we might not like them, because we want them to be intelligent but acquiescent. The power of many of the responsive environments in this book is precisely that they are not purely reactive or entirely predetermined. Both they and their users learn from experience and redefine their sense of place. In the process of their engagement they construct new meanings of personal as well as group significance.

CYBERNETIC SERENDIPITY
Exhibition poster
Designed by Franciszka Themerson
Curator Jasia Reichardt
Staged at the ICA, London, UK
1968

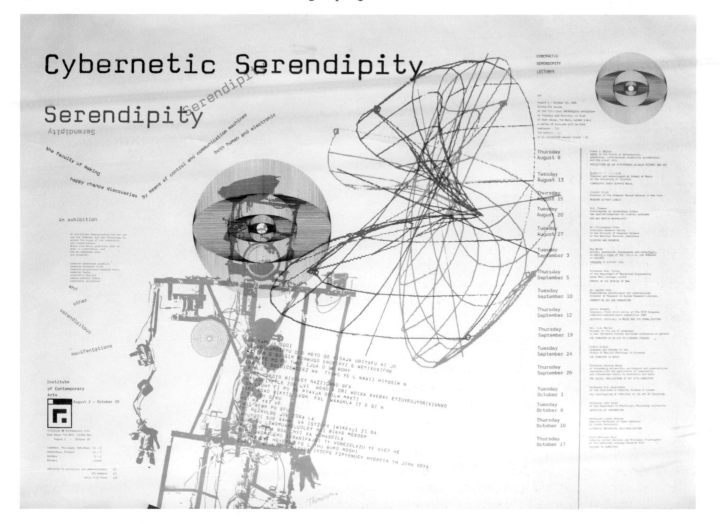

INTERACTIVE BUILDING SKINS

ONE OF THE MOST CREATIVE INNOVATIONS IN RESPONSIVE ARCHITECTURE HAS BEEN THE TREATMENT OF A BUILDING'S SURFACE AS AN INTERACTIVE SKIN.

TOWER OF WINDS
New shell for an old concrete tower
Toyo Ito
Yokohama, Japan
1986
Photos: Shinkenchiku-sha

One of the most creative innovations in responsive architecture has been the treatment of a building's surface as an interactive skin, onto and through which information and ambient effects can be streamed. An early programmable surface design was Buckminster Fuller's Pavilion Dome for the US at the 1967 Expo in Montreal. A shading device made of aluminium-coated fabric in triangular sections was arranged in groups of hexagons drawn and retracted by motors controlled by a punch-tape program (the method by which computer programs were stored in the 1960s). The surface-shading configuration changed every 20 minutes by following the path of the sun across the sky. This 'environmental valve', as Fuller called it, prefigured subsequent, more sophisticated mechanisms such as Jean Nouvel's Institute du Monde Arabe in Paris (1987–8; Nouvel was born in 1945, Fumel, France), which used retractable metal shading devices on the facade, responding to sunlight and ambient light levels.

In 1986 Japanese architect Toyo Ito (born Tokyo, Japan, 1941), who said he wanted to create architecture like an 'unstable flowing body', completed his '**TOWER OF WINDS**' in Yokohama.[25] Its kaleidoscope of colour and light is the result of the structure filtering the air, sounds and noises of the city, representing the visual complexity of Tokyo as a never-ceasing, ever-changing wind.

One of the first electronic media artworks to be applied to the facade of a building was Christian Moeller's 'KINETIC LIGHT SCULPTURE' installed in central Frankfurt in 1992, commissioned by a property developer looking for a concept for a light installation on the facade of the Zeilgalerie, a new shopping mall. The project was the biggest commission Moeller (born Frankfurt, 1959) had received to date. Designed to function only from twilight onwards, it entailed the facade being covered with a layer of perforated sheet metal. As dusk fell, this surface transformed itself into moving blue-yellow clusters of light, their patterns changing like a chameleon according to the weather. Three groups of lights, a total of 120 halogen spots mounted on catwalks, beamed from behind the metal sheet, were triggered to go on by twilight (and later off again by the coming of dawn). Each spotlight had a moveable lid that could be computer controlled to vary the light tones. At 0°C, the wall was monochrome blue, but as the temperature rose, yellow clusters would form. The direction of the wind monitored by the weather station on the roof caused the temperature-controlled colours to move across the wall. Near the top of the building Moeller and his team installed a 3 x 16-metre LED display screen showing the oscillating graphic renderings of the ambient sounds in the street. It had the appearance of a white line moving like an oscillograph to the sounds of the passers-by on the street. It was possibly the first interactive facade installation of this size ever built, and by day it operated as a news board.

Strangely, relatively few of the high-quality responsive surfaces designed by architects have been realized beyond the computer or at the scale of a model. dECOi, established in London and Paris in 1991 by UK architect Mark Goulthorpe (born Kent, UK, 1963), now professor in the department of architecture at MIT, USA, has a high level of engagement with digital technologies and collaborators such as Professor Mark Burry, a parametric design specialist as well as a robotics experts. Transcending static architecture or restrained planar forms to create elastic, kinetic counterparts, Goulthorpe subscribes to a more playful image of technology. In 1998 he won a competition to develop 'AEGIS HYPOSURFACE', the world's first 3-D responsive surface, an interactive real-time dynamic wall for the facade of the Birmingham Hippodrome Theatre in the UK. Not built due to the client's lack of funds, but shown in advanced prototype form at a European electronics fair and at the Pavillon de l'Arsenal, Paris, it had a matrix of actuators controlled by a computer that reacted in real time to voice and movement picked up electronically. This meant that it was capable of playing with passers-by, who found when they came close that their presence caused the surface to reconfigure. It effectively 'actualized the virtual of a new medium', as Goulthorpe put it.

KINETIC LIGHT SCULPTURE
Architects: Christian Moeller in collaboration with Rüdiger Kramm and Axel Strigl
Zeilgalerie, Frankfurt
Programming: Gideon May
Light design: Christian Bartenbach
Commissioned by Jürgen Schneider, developer
1992

'Paramorph' (meaning a body that can change its form while maintaining its properties), a proposal for the Gateway to the South Bank in London, was conceived as an interactive event space with a double skin of tessellated aluminium that drew light into the tunnel where it was sited as a form of opti-kinetic effect, with sound impacting on its surface texture. The installation encouraged people to engage with 'a ministry of silly walks', a playback device that registered change of movement, and imitated and encouraged interaction. One of Goulthorpe's favourite words is 'alloplastic', meaning a malleable and reciprocal relationship between the self and the environment.

The perception of architecture as relational and alloplastic has great implications for the built environment, provided that new propositions in this field fulfil their potential. This is a conceptual, technical and programmatic issue. The opening of the Kunsthaus in Graz, Austria, in 2003, designed by architects Peter Cook and Colin Fournier, presented a 900 square-metre outer skin called '**BIX**'[26] (big pixels) designed by the Berlin-based architects realities: united (directors: Jan and Tim Edler, born

BIX ELECTRONIC SKIN
Intelligent surface of the Kunsthaus,
Graz, Austria
realities: united (Jan and Tim Edler)
Architects: Peter Cook and Colin Fournier
2003
Photo: Angelo Kaunat

BIX ELECTRONIC SKIN
Intelligent surface of the Kunsthaus,
Graz, Austria
realities:united (Jan and Tim Edler)
Architects: Peter Cook and Colin Fournier
2003
Photo: Paul Ott, Graz

ONE OF GOULTHORPE'S FAVOURITE WORDS IS 'ALLOPLASTIC', MEANING A MALLEABLE AND RECIPROCAL RELATIONSHIP BETWEEN THE SELF AND THE ENVIRONMENT.

1970 and 1965, Cologne, Germany), integrating architecture, technology and visual message. Intended for use as an instrument and platform for artistic presentations, it is a part transparent, part opaque electronic membrane never previously realized in this form. Beneath the building's blue, bulbous acrylic facade on the side facing the river is an intermediate electronic membrane on top of a layer of mesh internal covering. Here, 930 circular fluorescent 40-watt light-ring tubes are integrated into each section of the facade, mounted in between the acrylic and the membrane.

'BIX' is actually quite a low-tech method. Using conventional big-screen display technology, and assuming the same budget, the surface area would have needed to be 100 times smaller. As a result, the resolution of the matrix is very low, with only 930 pixels, 0.2 per cent of the pixels in a conventional TV screen, and they are black and white, but the solution allows the design to be fully integrated into the architecture. Each ring of light functions as a pixel centrally controlled by computer. The lamps' brightness can be individually adjusted at an infinite variability with 20 frames per second, which allows images, films, animations and text to be displayed, transforming the Kunsthaus's skin into a giant, low-resolution computer display visible from a long distance.

LA DEFENSE
Office building facade
UN Studio
Almere Business Centre, the Netherlands
1999–2004
Commissioned by Eurocommerce, Deventer
Photos: Christian Richters

At night the outlines of the blue bubble become shadowy, and instead image sequences and varying text streams dance on its low-resolution screen, creating a stunning effect from across the river and vantage points around the city. realities: united see the relative coarseness and monochromacity of the visuals as an advantageous limitation, for new technology of large screens ages extremely fast, and this solution saves constant upgrading and costs. Software tools that evolved as part of the project were a key aspect of it (BIX Director, allowing the user to compose a program to be shown on the facade, and BIX Simulator, enabling artists to look at the results of their productions on a real-time 3-D computer simulation). reality:united's collaboration enables the building to transmit and radiate digital artworks like a clock tower. The light matrix is an amorphous zone tailored to the complex shape of the building, fading away at the edges, giving the impression that the bio-morphic shape creates the light patterns from within itself.

As a symbiotic part of this structure, 'BIX' enables the institution to present a transparency of information and content, and to further 'develop methods for dynamic communication between building and surroundings, between content and outside perception', as the architects explain. 'BIX' is a new medium in terms of resolution, scale, format and urban setting. Already artists like Shinsuke Kajitaka ('Waterfall', 2005) and Kentaro Taki ('Tentakle', 2005) have won competitions with their Quick Time movies for display on the Kunsthaus's facade. The building's fusion of architecture, design software and media technology offers architecture a new, mediated, responsive identity.

LA DEFENSE
Office building facade
UN Studio
Almere Business Centre, the Netherlands
1999–2004
Commissioned by Eurocommerce, Deventer
Photos: Christian Richters

Architectural techniques offering an apparent and ever-changing dematerialization of form can create multi-dimensional results, as the Dutch architects Ben van Berkel (born Utrecht, 1957) and Caroline Bos (born Rotterdam, 1959) discovered. Their practice, UN Studio, is a 'united network' of specialists and researchers not just in architecture, but also in urban development and infrastructure. A project recently completed in Almere in the Netherlands gave them the chance to put into action a material they had not previously used: a double multicoloured foil stretched to create a magnetic effect, and integrated in glass panels. They are now patenting the material and method after having tested it over a three-year period. **LA DEFENSE** (1999–2004), a part of OMA's urban plan in the city's Business Centre, is a 23,000 square-metre block of offices. It has a metallic facade that turns into nine different colours, letting people see a moiré colour shadow, and the impression that the building has an endless reflectiveness. 'Depending on the angle of incidence, the facade changes from yellow to blue, to red and from purple to green and back again,' says van Berkel. The building's form itself consists of four separate blocks of different lengths and heights with no other surface treatment, creating an integrated urban solution that is essentially closed apart from a link to the park at the rear. It is therefore an optimum formal solution for introducing what van Berkel calls the 'architecture of the after-image', with everything double reflecting. It is also a psychologically uplifting solution that avoids a visual flatness in brand identity.

DEPENDING ON THE ANGLE OF INCIDENCE, THE FACADE CHANGES FROM YELLOW TO BLUE, TO RED AND FROM PURPLE TO GREEN AND BACK AGAIN.

BEN VAN BERKEL

La Défense embodies UN Studio's interest in 'painting space'. Another recently completed building, the **GALLERIA HALL WEST** in the Apgujeong-dong district of Seoul, South Korea (2003–4), takes its cue from fashion's seasonal changes, with a light-reactive and programmable facade. A total of 4,330 glass disks with an iridescent foil are combined with a custom-designed lighting system created with Arup Lighting. This operates at night, reacting to the weather conditions throughout the day. A fast-track (ten-month) commission, it entailed UN Studio renovating an unremarkable existing building, streamlining circulation spaces into gallery-like 'catwalks' with walls. Outside, a grid system holds the sandblasted glass discs in three layers, so the surface of the building is a custom-designed skin. 'I wanted to create proliferating qualities to make it interactive and dynamic,' says van Berkel. 'We can test the malleability of colours almost as if we were de Chirico or Jeff Koons, and achieve both phenomenological and literal transparency.'

GALLERIA HALL WEST
Department store facade
UN Studio
Seoul, South Korea
Structural engineers: Arup & Partners
Lighting design: Arup Lighting/
Rogier van der Heide
Commissioned by Hanwha Stores Co., Ltd
2003–4

GALLERIA HALL WEST
Department store facade
UN Studio
Seoul, South Korea
Structural engineers: Arup & Partners
Lighting design: Arup Lighting/
Rogier van der Heide
Commissioned by Hanwha Stores Co., Ltd
2003–4

STORY PIPELINE
Installation
Ben Rubin
The BP Energy Center in Anchorage, Alaska
2002

UN Studio is designing further buildings that have an interactive relationship with their surroundings. A new theatre at Lelystad in the Netherlands, for instance, will have a reflective facade and 'inside-out' foyer, a dual strategy transforming the typical architectural box, opening it up to the world. Meanwhile Foreign Office Architects[27] plan to treat the south-facing facade of their future BBC Music Centre in west London as a broadcasting device, not via a bolted-on billboard, but as part of the banded form of the building, for which a layer of dichromatic 3M Radiant Mirror film is part of the triple-layered glass window. A grid of LED lights will reproduce the scenes of live music being played by the orchestras inside through an audio scan that converts it into digital patterns of colour and light streamed through the surface, giving it a chameleonic character.

Interactive elements are not always physically confined to a building's exterior. Ben Rubin's '**STORY PIPELINE**' artwork (2002) is located at the BP Energy Center in Anchorage, Alaska, a facility for use by community-based non-profit organizations.[28] Stories told by Alaskans appear on a plasma video screen and simultaneously emerge as real-time text transcriptions on a 150-foot long LED display. The text zigzags indoors down a glass corridor, then veers out through the plate glass facade, dancing between the trees until it disappears out of sight.

RESPONSIVE ARTWORKS

WITH TECHNOLOGIES WEAVING THEIR WAY INTO EVERYTHING, ARTISTIC PROJECTS THAT EXPLORE THE DOMAINS OF MIND AND BODY ADJUSTING TO ACCOMMODATE SUCH PHENOMENA ARE VITALLY RELEVANT.

With the pervasiveness of technologies weaving their way into everything from clothes tags to toilet seats, artistic projects that explore the subjective, personal domains of mind and body already adjusting to accommodate such phenomena are vitally relevant. In the context of urban environments – interfaces in their own right – their presence offers a medium of human investigation that is not hermetic, fixed or semiotic, but mutable and narrative based, giving technology an almost human and embodied presence. Many projects offer social commentary, and add a haptic layer to the environment that reads what is happening there, some more provocatively than others.

Although invisible radio-frequency ID (RFID) tags are becoming more common as a way of using new technologies to monitor shopping behaviour, responsive installations in public retail contexts are still a rarity. Instead, interactive programmes are confined to bringing in the punters via Jumbotrom screens in a cacophony of brand logos and advertising signboards that would drown out the impact of most of the more subtle artist- or architect-driven concepts.

LIGHT SOUNDS
Installation
d-squared (Clare Gerrard and Mark Hewitt)
with Rolf Gehlhaar
Sounds: Rolf Gehlhaar, Hagop Gehlhaar-
Matossian and META4
Light electronics: Interactive Imagination Ltd
N1 shopping centre, Islington,
North London, UK
Commissioned by Metro Shopping Fund
(Delancey and Land Securities Group plc),
2005

MULTI-DISCIPLINARY ENVIRONMENTS

Clare Gerrard (born Oxford, 1963) and Mark Hewitt (born London, 1962) run d-squared, a London-based architectural practice that encompasses art, product design and film. d-squared's '**LIGHT SOUNDS**' (2005), developed with installation artist Rolf Gehlhaar, transfers the multimedia solution typically found in interactive museum exhibits to the streetscape, creating an experiential attraction for shoppers, people visiting bars and clubs and other members of the public traversing the N1 shopping centre in Islington, north London. Set in a quiet zone of the centre, it registers the presence of passers-by, who trigger light and sound sequences depending on their numbers and behaviour. The pace of the changing coloured light and the tone and frequency of the sound are slow, so the sensation of passing the work is like moving past a highly abstracted electronic garden. To determine potential light and sound sequences, the group developed a generative structure that constantly renews itself, so that every time the sensors detect a visitor, a different sequence of lights and colours and a new constellation of sounds are triggered. The ultrasonic sensor system developed by Gehlhaar detects people's movements and triggers sound compositions. Some of the sounds were composed, others recorded in the city. These, d-squared explain, set up for onlookers a depth of association with concrete experiences and memories, urban and rural, which 'personalizes' the space, preferable to the effect of music made by others. 'Light Sounds' emerged from research into sensory installations rehearsed in earlier projects such as 'Thermochromic', an interactive children's resource centre that had nine mobile blocks coated in thermochromic paint, which could be reconfigured by the user. This highly sensitive surface engaged people and reacted to play by changing colour through the entire spectrum.

Data-driven interactive work does not need to be dry. It can create an almost subliminal impact in close proximity to transport infrastructure, viewed from the side of the road by fast-moving car drivers, for instance. '**LITMUS**' consists of five interactive installations on roundabouts along the A13 road; each is sited on a different site at Rainham Marshes in Essex, a post-industrial landscape and transitory place between a built-up area and marshland. The work was commissioned by Havering Borough Council and installed in 2004 by Jason Bruges (born Rochford, UK, 1972), one of a few practitioners in the UK making a full-time living from interactive installations applied within cultural and corporate contexts. Each installation is a 12 metre-high, stalk-like tower of transparent acrylic panels with a steel substructure and clusters of coloured LED lights above. 'They act as litmus papers, sensing and responding to their immediate environment, gathering information and displaying it to passing traffic.'

MY COMPOSITIONS ARE NOT COMPLETE WITHOUT THE INTERACTION OF AN INDIVIDUAL. EACH PERSON EXPERIENCING ONE OF MY WORKS WILL HAVE THEIR OWN UNIQUE MEMORY OF IT.
JASON BRUGES

LITMUS
Five interactive installations
Jason Bruges
Rainham Marshes, Essex UK,
on roundabouts along the A13 road
2004
Commissioned by London Borough of
Havering

Each installation employs light of a different colour, and thus serves as
an orientation device, with yellow adjusting to changing light levels,
orange to the tide level at Tilbury and royal blue to the amount of electricity generated by the neighbouring wind turbine. The green/blue
tower counts and displays the amount of traffic entering the Rainham
area. People can also view each installation remotely on a micro website
and change the parameters of the data source, which then affects the
sensors' algorithm technology online. Visually, the works are quite
abstract, but they are forever changing, a bit like the variable message
display system (VMD) used on motorways.

'I'm keen to hijack structures used for architecture and use them for art,'
says Bruges, who trained as an architect at Oxford Brookes University
and the Bartlett School of Architecture. His work explores the dynamic
and ephemeral qualities of light and interactivity, using self-illuminating
light technology or light projection that responds dynamically through
sensors to a range of stimuli. 'My compositions are not complete without
the interaction of an individual. Each person experiencing one of my
works will have their own unique memory of it,' says Bruges.

Relatively few architects focus wholly on responsive installations, co-opting artists' skills, but for those that do, their training lends them the confidence to apply their ideas at different scales. In urban environments, Christian Moeller is a consummate example of this. Born in Frankfurt (1959), he made Germany and later Linz in Austria his base until 2001, when he moved to Los Angeles to become a professor of design and media arts. He is one of many practitioners whose interests and opportunities stemmed from the media art scene. Trained as an architect, he began his career by working with Gunter Behnisch's architectural practice in the 1980s, but increasingly realized that the larger challenges lay in developing works with electronic media, which offered the opportunity to work with a wider variety of practitioners. In the late 1980s, Moeller became the first architect to have his own electronic media studio within an architectural practice. When his media architecture works using real-time phenomena became popular in the early 1990s, he stopped designing conventional buildings.

AUDIO GROVE
Installations
Christian Moeller
Composer: Ludiger Brümmer
Producer: Fumihiko Sumitomo
Light design: Nathan Thompson
1997
Commissioned by Spiral Gallery/
Wacoal Art Center (architect Fumihiko Maki), Tokyo, Japan
and exhibited at Sound Garden, Japan, 1997;
and at Cyber '98, Centro Cultural de Belém, Lisbon, Portugal

At the time, CAD had not yet been taken up by architecture, and it was long before desktop publishing made digital media activities affordable. A real-time video digitizing system cost around $90,000, far more than the comparative costs of today's desktop systems used in interactive design. Moeller was one of the first architecturally trained practitioners creating interactive spatial installations whose work could be found in a wide range of locations, from a shopping centre to a disused underground station and public spaces in the city. The majority of his projects are short term. They harness sound, light, weather conditions, movements of the body and human emotions, creating spaces that are not only responsive and manipulable, but also accessible and often humorous.

'AUDIO GROVE' was one of three sound installations commissioned by the Spiral Gallery/Wacoal Art Center in Aoyama, Tokyo (architect Fumihiko Maki), staged in 1997 with composer Ludiger Brümmer. Installed below a huge skylight, 64 upright iron poles almost 6 metres high were linked to touch-sensitive electronic sensors. When touched by a visitor, they emitted sounds as the impact triggered the audio system. One simple touch activated one sound, and the simultaneous touch of two poles moved the overall audio up or down by one octave. Brümmer used a physical modelling system to create the most resonant sound elements. 'He engineers virtual objects as instruments (on computer), locates them in a mathematically constructed virtual world and designs the attack to create a particular sound,' explains Moeller. The installation's touch sensitivity was also harnessed to light for the installation, with 25 spotlights aligned into place. When the poles were touched, the lights went on and off alternately, generating what Moeller calls 'a light shadow texture' on the floor like a carpet. The installation became a popular meeting point where people had fun creating effects with the light sensors, and one that was very atmospheric at night.

BODY MOVIES: RELATIONAL ARCHITECTURE 6
Projection
Rafael Lozano-Hemmer
2002
Commissioned by V2 and staged at the
Schouwburgplein, Rotterdam, the Netherlands, 2002;
during Cultural Capital of Europe, Rotterdam;
Sapphire 02, Lisbon, Portugal;
Ars Electronica, 2002, Linz, Austria;
Liverpool Biennial 2002, UK;
and Duisburg Akzente, 2003, as well as in Seoul,
Sao Paulo and Singapore

Rafael Lozano-Hemmer is a media artist whose ground-breaking project 'Relational Architecture', a series of large-scale interventions in public spaces initiated in 1997, used custom-made technologies to transform urban space. Situated between architecture and the performing arts, his usually temporary projects explore relationships between a site and the public, creating a range of collective social experiences. Working with photographers, programmers, architects, linguists, writers, composers, actors and other specialists, he identifies two common forms of collective interactivity. The first involves one or two sensors, and people take turns using them; the rest are spectators. In the second, input is computed according to averages. The challenge is to avoid either of these modes. Lozano-Hemmer feels his work '**BODY MOVIES: RELATIONAL ARCHITECTURE 6**', shown at the Schouwburgplein in Rotterdam in 2002, did this. He prefers to call 'the act of seeing the act of inventing'. The work involved projecting the shadows of passers-by, which were then detected by a single camera tracker. People knew the moving shadow projected onto buildings was clearly their own, and they played roles to further lend the piece imaginative force. Patterns emerged when groups were present and chose to interact with each other in different ways.

Instead of creating clichéd special effects, the piece used shadows to generate reflection on the idea of embodiment, disembodiment and what spectacular representation might be. It also worked with the idea of distance between bodies in public space, reinterpreting the 'daily urban performance' in a way that allowed opportunities for self-representation. 'Body Movies' was shown in many different cities, including Linz, Liverpool, Seoul, Sao Paulo and Singapore, giving Lozano-Hemmer the chance to cross-reference the variety of behaviours emerging in different settings.

Relational architecture, according to Lozano-Hemmer, means transforming the representational narratives of buildings by adding and subtracting audio-visual elements which autonomously demonumentalize their identity in urban contexts. His most recent projects are also about exchange. 'Subtitled Public', presented at El Cubo, in the Sala de Arte Publico Siqueiros in Mexico City in 2005, consisted of an empty exhibition space where visitors were tracked with a computerized infrared surveillance system. As people entered the installation, texts were projected onto their bodies, 'subtitles' with thousands of verbs conjugated in the third person that followed the individual everywhere they went. The only way to get rid of a subtitle was to touch someone else: the words were then exchanged between them. This piece is a good comment on surveillance systems that typecast and try to detect different ethnic groups, and more widely on the implications of technological personalization that literally 'themes' or 'brands' an individual a consumer.

SUBTITLED PUBLIC
Installation
Rafael Lozano-Hemmer
Presented in the Dataspace exhibition,
Conde Duque Art Center, Madrid, 2005;
El Cubo, in the Sala de Arte Publico Siqueiros,
Mexico City, 2005; and Cultural Capital of Europe,
Luxembourg, 2007
Produced by BBVA-Bancomer Foundation, Mexico City
Photo: Alex Dorfsman

Lozano-Hemmer has also designed a pioneering responsive environment – 'SURFACE TENSION' (1991–4) – which has now been acquired by museums and collectors in Mexico, London, Miami and Zurich. Intended to illuminate the boundary between the virtual and the real, it employs custom-made technology led by an ultrasonic wand input device, inter-active animation and music, both triggered by dance. For each of the three acts of the performance, which is carried out by dancers and then by the audience, there is an electronic environment. The first is about surveillance. A huge eye observes the person on stage. The dancers, who wear the ultrasonic wand, can control its blinking and expressions. Then a virtual 3-D map lets the wand trigger and control words and sentences in sampled sound and in an enormous animated mouth, so the dancers can actually create speech. Thirdly, the index finger of a very large fist follows the person on stage, gesturing 'not you!' or 'you're OK'. The wand gives very precise computer data about the dancer's position, velocity and acceleration around the stage, responding to even minute movements, generating music and affecting computer animation in real time. The dancer becomes the mouse for a network of computers. Lozano-Hemmer explains that we are accustomed to a media interface being superficial, in the form of a screen, but here, by visualizing the interface and providing the means to literally grab it with a wand, he hopes 'to cause a disturbance in the way we understand cyberspace'.

LOZANO-HEMMER 'HOPES TO CAUSE A DISTURBANCE IN THE WAY WE UNDERSTAND CYBERSPACE.'

While Moeller, an émigré, is now one of the US's best-known interactive artists, Lozano-Hemmer is active in Canada and Mexico (his country of birth), as well as internationally. The American continent has been fertile territory for responsive environments, fostered both within academia and on the art scene.

The Rockefeller new media fellowship is one of a tiny handful supporting this type of work. The new-media organization Eyebeam, in New York, which operates on the atelier model with studios and workspaces, wants to create new premises in the near future.[29] Practitioners have created many of the contemporary interactive spatial installations by Americans shown in recent years with roots in the performing arts or film. Jim Campbell's cinematic inspired works, and Grahame Weinbren's early film interactive design from the 1980s, have influenced younger practitioners. Paul Kaiser, an artist who works with large projections, often uses dancers and makes live performances.

SURFACE TENSION
Installation
Collaboration with Transition State Theory
with the assistance of Bruce Ramsay and
Tara DeSimone
Rafael Lozano-Hemmer
1991–4
Exhibited at 2M, Madrid, Spain, 1993,
SIGGRAPH, Anaheim, USA, 1993; Akademie
der Bildenden Künste, Nüremberg, Germany,
1993; and OMR Gallery, Mexico, 2004
Photo: Celina Roig

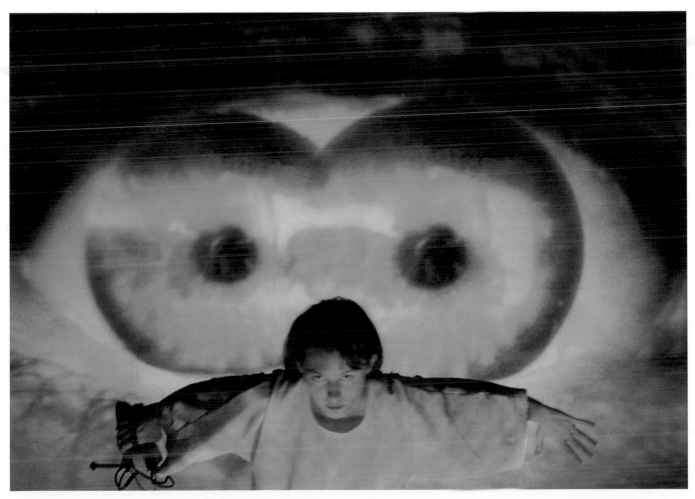

Ben Rubin (born Boston, 1964), who took his Masters at MIT Media Lab, set up EAR Studio in 1993.[30] 'My intention was to create a small-scale framework to continue research and experiments in media arts as I had been doing at MIT.' Earlier on much of his work was for theatre and performance, developing interactive staging, sound and projection projects. The other side of EAR's work was creating interactive exhibitions and environments for Manhattan museums like the American Museum of the Moving Image, the Smithsonian and the Whitney. The activities in these fields gave Rubin, in time, the space to create his own body of art installations. Now, these have taken a central role in the studio, and the projects have grown in scale from gallery work to building-scale public art in corporate headquarters and a 150-foot LED sign outside a commercial centre in Alaska (see page 29).

'**BLUR**', one of three pavilions at the 2002 Swiss Expo at Yverdon-les-Bains in Switzerland, was one of EAR Studio's major collaborations with New York architects Diller and Scofidio (Elisabeth Diller, born 1954, Lodz, Poland and Ricardo Scofidio, born 1935, New York, USA), well known for creating projects including animations and exhibitions commissioned by museums and galleries. EAR created the media and interactive elements of 'Blur', an artificial cloud 300 feet wide by 200 feet deep floating 75 feet above a lake. Situated in the Three Lakes region above Lausanne, it was a modest structure rather than a monumental pavilion boasting national feats. A metal space frame a bit like an oil rig was suspended over the water. It was studded with over 31,000 tiny nozzles and contained a skeletal weather-making machine producing a perpetually changing blanket of fog. Enveloped by the mist, intrepid visitors – up to 400 could enter the building at any one time – arriving at the structure's platform from the 120 metre-long access bridge, had to work out how to function in a sometimes disorienting environment devoid of visual information. They filled in a Dada-style questionnaire in advance, and the data was fed into a computer linked to each of their 'braincoats'– plastic raincoats that turned red or green at the whim of the master computer. Movements towards or away from other participants triggered an electronic reaction, blushing red, for instance. If two raincoats reacted in the same way, they reflected an affinity between their wearers.

The effect was of a kind of social radar, 'producing anonymous or involuntary intimacy'. 'Could these wireless, unfixed technologies expand communication beyond conventional language? Transmit emotions, attractions or embarrassment?' Diller asks. Drenched by clouds of spume, the mystified participants strolled in their 'braincoats', laughing out loud at the sheer audacity and spontaneity of the performance they had just walked into – and become a key part of.

COULD THESE WIRELESS, UNFIXED TECHNOLOGIES EXPAND COMMUNICATION BEYOND CONVENTIONAL LANGUAGE? TRANSMIT EMOTIONS, ATTRACTIONS OR EMBARRASS-MENT?
ELISABETH DILLER

BLUR
Pavilion
Diller+Scofidio (architects);
Steve Rubin of EAR Studio
(interactive design)
2002

Diller + Scofidio's architecture is a performance that demands participation. As Diller explains, 'We are specifically interested in the convergence of electronics and architecture, and in the immersive potential of "Blur", beyond the mechanisms of the eye, and on an environmental scale. Entering is like coming into a habitable medium, except that orientation is lost and time suspended. It is like being immersed in ether.' More than two years in the planning, 'Blur' survived numerous problems that threatened to dilute the thrust of the architects' carefully engineered innovations, from contaminated water to over-zealous building inspectors who wanted to install a sprinkler system. Despite being completed without its planned light- and sound-based communication systems after the buyout of a corporate sponsor, 'Blur' was acclaimed an environmental masterpiece, even though it only lasted one summer.

'Blur' also incorporated what could be called 'smart weather' – a computer interpreted the changing weather conditions and then ordered the production of more or less fog, as required to cover the building. It was not the first fog building: that distinction belongs to the geodesic dome covered by a fog-like layer created by Japanese artist Fujoko Nakiya for the Osaka World's Fair in 1970, but 'Blur' used fog to do away with architecture's traditional reliance on tectonic form and the facade as a means of representation. It stands at the intersection of media and landscape by combining nature and artifice into a new hybrid condition.

HYBRID SONIC-VISUAL-HAPTIC WORKS

Ben Rubin's most celebrated work is the collaborative visual and sonic piece '**THE LISTENING POST**', based on explorations of the communication flows in Internet chat rooms and forums. Exhibited at the Brooklyn Academy of Music, Next Wave Festival, 2001, and other venues in the US and in Paris,[31] it was developed with statistician Mark Hansen. It gives vocal form via voice synthesizer to fragments from the array of conversations in Internet chat rooms, bulletin boards and other public forums while simultaneously displaying them across a suspended grid of over 200 small electronic screens. Chat data is received in real time, so that the irregular staccato of these arriving messages forms the visual and audible rhythms of the work. The piece works its way through a series of six movements, each a different arrangement of visual, aural and musical elements, with its own processing logic.

THE LISTENING POST
Installation
Ben Rubin and Mark Hansen, 2001–4
Exhibited at the Brooklyn Academy of Music,
Next Wave Festival, New York, 2001;
the Whitney Museum of American Art, 2002;
MIT List Visual Arts Center, 2004, USA;
and La Villette, Paris, France
2004
Photo p.42: courtesy of the artist
Photo p.43: David Allison

THE LISTENING POST
Installation
Ben Rubin and Mark Hansen, 2001–4
Exhibited at the Brooklyn Academy of Music,
Next Wave Festival, New York, 2001;
the Whitney Museum of American Art, 2002;
MIT List Visual Arts Center, 2004, USA;
and La Villette, Paris, France
2004
Photo: courtesy of the artist

In the process of development Rubin had as much input in data collection and modelling as Hansen did on questions of design and aesthetics. They identified the emotional qualities of chat, from which a kind of music began to emerge. The audience was invited to watch and listen to the piece, but not directly intervene, generally reacting emotionally to the content itself. Many viewers felt it reinforced a sense of a collective global community.

Sonic-visual works, if they work well, are also fine-tuned to be haptic in unexpected ways. One of Rubin's much earlier interactive sound installations, 'Soundplay', from 1993 (initially exhibited in the summer of 1993 at the Nickle Arts Museum in Calgary[32]), translated the slightest movement of the feet, bending of the knees, and even the movement of a head or hand, into sound. Through experimentation, a visitor could discover a posture from which the contraction of a single thigh muscle articulated a melody, or another in which raising and lowering one's arm would shift a set of tones resonating with the surrounding ambience. 'The immediacy of the aural feedback could result in an almost trance-like state of attentiveness to the smallest movements of one's body,' says Rubin.

THE IMMEDIACY OF THE AURAL FEEDBACK COULD RESULT IN AN ALMOST TRANCE-LIKE STATE OF ATTENTIVENESS TO THE SMALLEST MOVEMENTS OF ONE'S BODY.
BEN RUBIN

The piece, a simple metre-square wooden platform sensitive to the amount and the position of force (weight) applied to it, was connected to a computer continuously interpreting force measurements. Sound was generated, modulated or processed in response to changes in the measured forces, and played via four speakers suspended around the platform at each corner, directed at the centre of the room. The sounds produced varied according to methods and parameters set up within the computer program. Some of the sound programs were musical and rhythmic, using piano, cello and bell sounds; others created virtual environments, in which the visitors' motions elicited, for example, human breathing and heartbeats, or allowed their makers to splash around in a virtual stream.

Maywa Denki (1993 –), a Japanese art duo, have questioned whether such installations are functional or nonsense machines, to this end creating an entire exhibition of 'Nonsense Machines' at ICC in Tokyo in 2004. Masamichi and Nobumichi Tosa (born Hyogo, Japan, 1965 and 1967) are artists who make products and stage performances. Their 'TSUKUBA' series, included in the exhibition, consisted of musical 'devices' played via the physical movement at 100 volts of motors and electromagnets. They called the sounds 'machine music materially performed by electric-powered musical instruments'.

While the 'Nonsense Machines' engaged through sound and the novelty of kineticism alone, converting sound into image through a powerful aesthetic metaphor – when it works – is immensely revealing. **'ARTIFACTS OF THE PRESENCE ERA'** was a work designed by the ICA Boston Media Department and the Sociable Media Group at the MIT Media Laboratory (Fernanda Viégas, Ethan Perry, Ethan Howe and Judith Donath). A Web camera and a microphone captured a myriad of images and sounds and then every five minutes visualized them as yet another layer in a growing, organic landscape accumulating like the layers of a canyon. This aesthetic geological metaphor then guided the way in which the historic essence of the piece was manifested. The shape of each layer depended on audio peaks and troughs of ambient noise, and variance in colour on changes in ambient light and the movement of visitors in the gallery. As more information accumulated at the top, earlier layers became compressed and less distinct. Visitors used a control knob to navigate up and down the stack of layers, and each time it became highlighted, the image from that layer and the time the layer was created were shown on the right side of the display. 'Instead of viewing our piece as an isolated effort to represent the passage of time in a museum, we believe that our visualization approach and design lessons have implications for personally or collectively meaningful databases, ranging from video footage in personal webcams to newsgroups' conversation,' say the team. As the contents of digital archives permeating our daily lives become more emotionally charged with the accretion of all the computer-mediated conversations people have with their loved ones over email and digital pictures, the pleasures of data analysis are the only motivation for visualizing massive collections of documents. 'Artifacts' shifts the perception of such archives from being merely data repositories to one of powerful catalysts for memory.

ARTIFACTS OF THE PRESENCE ERA
Installation
ICA Media Department and the Sociable
Media Group at the MIT Media Laboratory
(Fernanda Viégas, Ethan Perry, Ethan Howe
and Judith Donath)
Exhibited at ICA, Boston, USA
2003

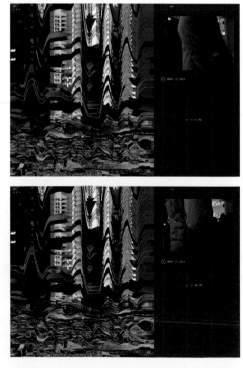

CINEMATIC PLAYTIME WITH IMAGE AND SOUND

BOUNDARY FUNCTIONS
Installation
Scott Snibbe
Exhibited at Ars Electronica
1998
On permanent installation at the Phaeno
Science Centre, Wolfsburg, Germany
(architect Zaha Hadid)
and at Saigomax, Vietnam
Previously exhibited at Ars Electronica,
Austria, 1998, NTT ICC, Tokyo, 1999
and many other international venues
Photo: Kris Snibbe

Film as a cultural medium has deeply influenced many responsive environments. American artist Scott Snibbe (born New York City, 1969) is one of a number of practitioners who trained as experimental film-makers and animators. '**BOUNDARY FUNCTIONS**', created in 1998, has since 2005 been permanently set up at the Phaeno Science Centre (architect Zaha Hadid) in Wolfsburg, Germany and at Saigomax in Vietnam. It is a deft demonstration of the fact that personal space exists and changes only in relation to others without our control. A set of lines projected by an overhead camera through an intermediate mirror onto a retro-reflective floor divides each person from the next in a series of cellular spaces. As people move, the 'net' changes but always describes each person's individual space, maintaining an even distance.

DEEP WALLS
Installation
Scott Snibbe
2003
Commissioned by San Francisco Museum
of Modern Art (Media Art Coalition)
Exhibition venues include SFMOMA, USA, 2003;
Ars Electronica, 2003, Korea; and Art Interactive,
USA, 2005
Photos: Scott Snibbe

The defined spaces surrounding each person are based on the mathe-matical concept of Voronoi diagrams, or Dirichlet tessellations.[33] 'In this installation a mathematical abstraction is made instantly knowable by dynamic visual representation,' says Snibbe. Unlike the more hermetic effects of virtual reality, this is a virtual space that can only exist with more than one person. It works through the connection of the camera and projector to a computer that tracks the people moving below by process-ing the video image using custom software; that software then generates the Voronoi diagram, which is then projected back onto the floor.

Another of Snibbe's works, **'DEEP WALLS'** (2003), 'collects' viewers' shadows on a retro-reflective screen. Their movements are projected, played back repeatedly and reduced to a rectangle one-sixteenth the size of the screen. Each collected shadow film has the precise duration of its recording. Initially, when a viewer or viewers move in front of the screen and their shadows start to be recorded, one box is cleared out. The work offers up records of movements within the space, organizes and collects them onto flat projections. 'Deep Walls' gradually absorbs the contents of its environment onto its surface.

MY WORKS
REWARD
VIEWERS WITH
AN IMMEDIATE,
VISCERAL SENSE
OF PRESENCE,
WHILE
SIMULTANEOUSLY
INDUCING THEM
TO UNDERSTAND
THE CONCEPTUAL
MOTIVATION
AND DEEPER
MEANING
BEHIND THE
WORK.
SCOTT SNIBBE

Snibbe's work portrays through bodily interactions the interdependence of individuals with their environments and with each other. Most of his projects do not function unless viewers actively engage with them by touching, breathing or moving in their vicinity. Also, although they use new technologies, his viewers' experiences usually take place as human-to-human interactions. He describes his working process as subtractive, 'removing elements until only those necessary for conveying a work's meaning remain'. Phenomenology, or the philosophy of how the body 'thinks' through unmediated perception rather than through reason and language, also gives his projects a strong foundation. Much like most of the works in this book, participants do not get handed meaning 'on a plate'; they construct the meaning of his works through a process of physical awareness, which philosopher Merleau-Ponty (1908–61) has said 'gives us at every moment a global, practical and implicit notion of the relation between our body and things, of our hold on them'. [34] Snibbe's works fulfil a responsive agenda in this sense, because they 'reward viewers with an immediate, visceral sense of presence, while simultaneously inducing them to understand the conceptual motivation and deeper meaning behind the work,' explains the artist.

Emerging European interactive designers', young artists', and architects' fields and means of exploration have led away from the preservation of disciplinary or national boundaries, for many reasons to do with converging media, common interests and a desire to share knowledge bases. Self-organization, an internationalist approach, interdisciplinary collaboration, and a commitment to open prototyping and scientific research are pronounced new features of the ways in which they work.

NEW PRACTICE IDENTITIES AND STRATEGIES

THERE ARE ARTISTS LIKE SNIBBE, WHO TRAINED IN COMPUTER SCIENCE, ART AND EXPERIMENTAL ANIMATION, AND DIVIDES HIS TIME BETWEEN TEACHING, RESEARCH POSITIONS AND MAKING MEDIA INSTALLATIONS.

BRUIT ROSE (PINK NOISE)
Installation
HeHe Association
(Helen Evans and Heiko Hansen)
2004
Installed in Rue Rosier, Saint-Ouen, 2004,
as part of Art Grandeur Nature; the Biennial
of Contemporary Art of Seine-St Denis,
and on Witte de Withstraat, Rotterdam,
the Netherlands, as part of Hands On
Hands Off: Three Surfaces of Disengagement,
V2, Rotterdam, the Netherlands

On the one hand, there are artists like Snibbe, who trained in computer science, art and experimental animation, and divides his time between teaching media art and experimental film, holding research positions at Adobe and Interval, and making electronic media installations that have been widely shown. On the other, there are young designers who tend to team up more formally in a group in order to create their multi-disciplinary works. In rare cases they forge an institutional identity. HeHe is such a case. Named after the first two letters of their first names, HeHe is co-run by Helen Evans (born Welwyn Garden City, UK, 1972) and Heiko Hansen (born Pinneberg, Germany, 1970), with its studio base in St Ouen since 2002, a suburb to the north of Paris. It is an independent non-profit making organization for the creation of art and design projects that intersect with interactive technologies. This structure allows Evans and Hansen to pursue their own research agenda and to participate in projects, events and lectures within contexts relating to divergent disciplines including art, design, architecture and scientific research. Many of their projects are collaborative, working with research laboratories, academia or commissions from cultural centres. Their autonomy is important for the duo: 'practising artists or designers are very rarely asked to drive the themes of scientific or cultural research within larger institutions', says Evans.

'In French film, architecture and art there is a rich cultural tradition that explores ideas of responsive architecture,' says Evans, recalling the films of Jacques Tati, particularly 'Playtime' and 'Mon Oncle', which explore the humorous and surreal potential of an automated, electronically mediated world. Evans notes that the idea of using office windows as an interactive element for large-scale images in the city can be spotted in 'Playtime'. Another French precursor who has influenced HeHe's ideas is the exuberant architect and cybernetic pioneer Nicolas Schoffer (1912–1992), who built many large, utopian structures that responded to the environment. Besides his many realized works, such as the 50 metre-high 'Spatiodynamic Cybernetic Sound Tower', built in Paris in 1954 with the collaboration of sound artist Pierre Henry, the most intriguing is his unrealized 'Cybernetic Light Tower' for the La Défence quarter of Paris, proposed in 1970. The 307 metre-high tower was to support a structure of pivoting mirrors and spotlights that turned in all directions. It was also to be programmed to react in real time to its immediate environment and to remote information, from the temperature of the River Seine to the current fluctuations on the stock market.

There has been much interactive experimentation recently in France, and the field is strengthened by the presence of two networks, one based around a small company called Interface-Z, which develops electronic sensors for artists internationally; and Art Sensitif, a non-profit association that runs educational workshops and a resource centre for real-time technologies. There are as yet very few artistic courses that teach students the technical skills required to realize complex projects. However, according to Evans, 'there is an increasing amount of institutional interest for these types of project, so things are changing'.

HeHe's work uses installation as a means to explore the way in which people can read, write and reinterpret their urban and architectural environment. The duo is critical of how they see embedded and pervasive technologies being used for a narrow set of objectives: to monitor, watch, count and control. Their works aim to expand the possible objectives and in consequence the social and aesthetic effects of pervasive technologies. Their interactive language focuses on environments that are both functional and reflective, which act like a mirror, sending back the protagonist a filtered, transformed representation of the self. Many of their projects establish new relationships between artwork, observers and the urban context. 'Lofi', for instance, transforms the image of a 1950s' corporate facade into a hi-fi graphic equalizer signalling the sound levels of concerts to residents and people queuing outside the venue. '**BRUIT ROSE**' (Pink Noise) 'advertises' noise levels in a busy street, turning a transmitter of desire into a receptor responding to the everyday sounds of cars and passers-by. Installed within a light box on the street usually used for advertising in Saint-Ouen in 2004 (and in Rotterdam in 2005), it visualizes ambient sounds, including those of passers-by. The box's light-emitting panels are commonly used to convey formatted advertising, but here they work as an animated visual, receiving and relaying in another medium what happens in the immediate environment.

THEIR CONCEPTS OFFER NEW WAYS OF INTERACTING, INTEGRATED INTO FORMS THAT PEOPLE RECOGNIZE, FROM SALAD BOXES THAT BECOME LAMPS, TO GRAPHIC EQUALIZERS THAT PLAY ON FACADES, OR CHIMNEY FUMES THAT BECOME ENVIRONMENTAL BAROMETERS.

POLLSTREAM – NUAGE VERT (GREEN CLOUD)
Laser projection and public advertising
campaign
HeHe Association (Helen Evans and
Heiko Hansen)
Installed at the waste-burning plant,
Saint-Ouen, France; and at Salmisaar power
plant, Ruoholahti Harbour, Helsinki, Finland,
as part of PixelAche Festival
2005

HeHe's proposal '**POLLSTREAM – NUAGE VERT**' (Green Cloud, 2005) evolves this theme of architecture as a broadcaster of real-time dynamic data. 'Nuage Vert' uses lasers and a camera-tracking system to project colour-coded information onto a waste-burning plant/tower within local areas that is visible to all residents. The moving plume changes colour, showing levels of energy being consumed at any given time; the chimney becomes a community measuring tape or shared canvas. This is an important distinction, since the architecture becomes more than a passive representation of information, setting up a participatory relationship with its audience. In '**LIGHT BRIX**' (see page 54), a modular wall of light, each lamp will gradually turn on or off when touched, inviting people to draw or imprint their mark onto the space.

Rather than abstracting their concepts into new forms, HeHe borrow from a common visual language within everyday life and accessible without prior knowledge. Their concepts offer new ways of interacting, integrated into forms that people recognize, from salad boxes that become lamps, to graphic equalizers that play on facades, or chimney fumes that become environmental barometers. Reappropriating common signs and objects in culture, HeHe transform them with a new social function.

LIGHT BRIX
Lighting system
HeHe Association
(Helen Evans and Heiko Hansen) with Graham Plumb,
2001
Produced during Research Fellowship at Interaction Design Institute Ivrea, Italy
Batch produced by monofunction, Z-Interface for Federico de Giuli and AB+, Turin

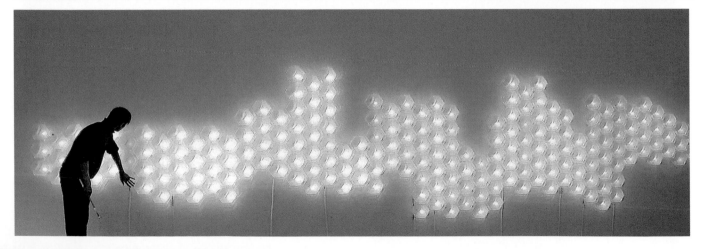

MIRROIR AUX SILHOUETTES (MIRROR SPACE)

Two-way tele-presence system
HeHe (Helen Evans and Heiko Hansen) with
In Situ research laboratory LR1 + INRI Futurs
2002
Part of the Disappearing Computer/Future &
Emerging Technologies research programme
initiated by the EU. Exhibited in various
galleries in Paris, France; at Design Interactif,
Pompidou Centre, Paris, France, 2003;
and at La Villette Numérique: Emergences,
Cité de Sciences et de l'Industries, Paris,
France, 2004

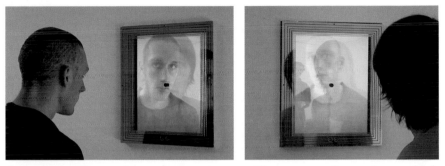

As in Jason Bruges's work, the site-specific aspect of a project, which could be quite a rough street space, is important to the way HeHe proceed. For example, their '**MIRROR SPACE**' (2002) is a two-way tele-presence installation designed to support multiple levels of communication – public, personal, close and intimate. To realize this work, a digital camera was reverse engineered to be as small as possible and then fixed in place, in the centre of a portrait screen. This detail appears imperceptible to people, since they are often preoccupied with looking at themselves and the other person in the mirror, but it allows for a fundamental form of non-verbal communication to take place: eye contact between remote persons.

Three cultural environments heavily influenced HeHe's creative direction. The Computer Related Design Department (CRD), now renamed the Interaction Design Department under the direction of Tony Dunne, at the Royal College of Art, offered a culture based on the idea of 'interaction' as a field of exploration in relation to people and technology. CRD was launched long before the word became overused, acting consciously as a parallel to MIT Media Lab, with its model of rapid prototyping leading to innovation. It emphasized the overlapping agendas of art, design and research rather than science. It was a proponent of the idea of technology as a medium that is both material and immaterial, and therefore has important social and aesthetic effects. At Mains d'Oeuvres, in St Ouen, HeHe were artists in residence (2002–4) alongside other emerging artists: musicians, dancers, graphic designers, social activists and visual artists. This space offered many opportunities to discuss, experiment and show work to a very broad public. Finally, HeHe have worked at various science oriented research laboratories (Frauenhofer in Germany, Project In Situ in France). This has exposed them to scientific research methods, inspiring them to formulate their own research questions.

SOCIALLY MODULATED LANDSCAPE
Interactive video project
José Gonçalo Alves and Sara Inglês Lopes,
with Ivan Franco and Cristina Dias, 2005
Exhibited in S'Cool Ibérica, Cordoaria
Nacional–Torreão Nascente,
ExperimentaDesign 2005, Lisbon, Portugal
Photo: Paul Makovsky

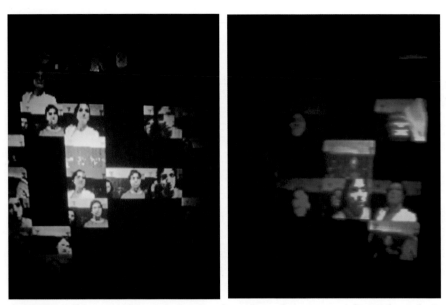

Architects have made prototypes of mediated spaces to formulate their own research questions through works such as Vicente Guallart's collaborative 'Media House',[35] and more recently the '**INDUCTION HOUSE**', designed by Adam Somlai-Fischer, a young Hungarian architect who runs aether architecture.[36] Unlike 'Media House', 'Induction House' prototypes are less to do with domestic occupation than about the opportunity to explore hybrid construction and a new relationship between technology and design based on complexity theory. The Czech philosopher Vilém Flusser (1920–1991), one of the most important media theorists of recent years, believed that 'what we perceive as reality is a tiny detail from the field of possibilities surging around us, which our nervous system has realized through computation. If all reality is a computation from possibilities, then 'reality' is a 'threshold' value'.[37] Somlai-Fischer, a teacher at the Architecture and Urban Research Laboratory KTH Stockholm, [38] wants architects to look more closely at the implications of this, and in particular the fact that electronic media saturate our cultural environment, influencing our perceived reality.

THROUGH CONSTANT REAP-PROPRIATION OF EXISTING TECHNOLOGIES WE CREATE NEW INTERFACES THAT CONNOTE THEIR ORIGINAL USE AND HAVE SOME FAMILIARITY, BUT ARE ALSO MISPLACED IN A NEW CONTEXT.
ADAM SOMLAI-FISCHER

INDUCTION HOUSE – THE FISHING KIT

Architectural prototype
(the first two were 'The Fish Tank' and
'Distributed Projection Structure')
aether architecture (Adam Somlai-Fischer,
Péter Hudini, Anita Pozna, Bengt Sjölén)
Exhibited at the Kunsthalle Budapest, 2003
(prototype 1); Kiasma Centre for
Contemporary Art, Pixelache festival,
Helsinki, Finland, 2004 (prototype 2);
ISEA2004, Helsinki, Finland; and Gallery U,
Hungarian Cultural Institute, Helsinki

Somlai-Fischer asked himself what new architecture could arise from our rapidly developing technological environment. He decided to test new possibilities, not with the representational methods of plans and sections, as in a regular architectural project, but by building prototypes on a one-to-one scale that blur the electronic media into the physical space. Investigating ways of treating digital media as physical matter, the surface of a computer projection is unfolded onto a translucent structure, with the result that 'layers of digital information, behaviour and ambience share projection territories' and create the prospect of a 'non-screen-based computer environment'. The first prototype was a 100 x 100 x 60-centimetre structure of steel and textiles, based on an algorithm that is a sliced flat plane folded, creating a 100 per cent projectable continuous surface. An electromagnetic field sensor senses mobile phone usage, and a set of light sensors the shadows of hands. The mobile phone calls change the electronic weather or projected colour temperature, a process not unlike that employed in Usman Haque's 'Sky Ear' project (see page 63). By the time it was shown in its second version (V2) at pixelACHE at the Kiasma Museum of Contemporary Art,

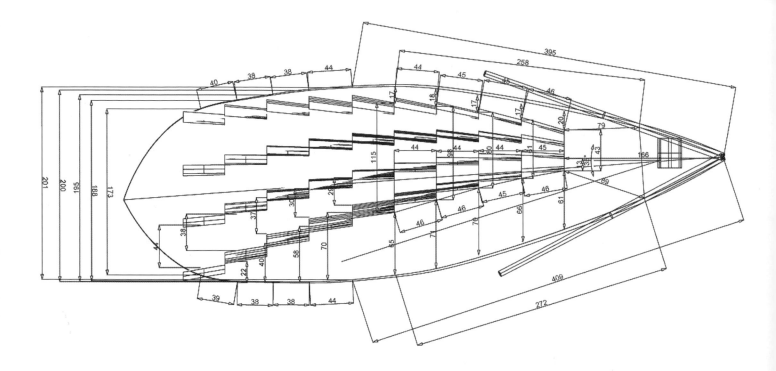

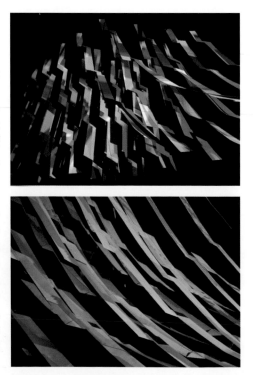

Helsinki in April 2004,[39] the structure was much larger, 600 x 300 x 170 centimetres, with 300 physical pixels in a matrix that moved along the projectors' light, creating a 100 per cent projectable volumetric structure. Ultrasonic sensors measured visitors' presence and distance. These first two incarnations used Flash as a projection engine and, to interface this program to sensors, a microcontroller clicking Morse signals on a USB computer mouse. The team initially used these low-tech solutions out of necessity, and then as a choice. 'Through constant reappropriation of existing technologies we create new interfaces that connote their original use and have some familiarity, but are also misplaced in a new context'.

More recently, in the autumn of 2004, 'Induction House V3' was an 800 x 400 x 200-centimetre carbon fibre, steel and plastic structure with 400 analogue pixel folds that worked outdoors in the sunshine, using solar power and radio communication, its spatial flows sensing and changed by approaching visitors (media designed by Bengt Sjölén, a gaming technology researcher). Somlai-Fischer put all the chronological stages of the development process – interaction, physical design, technology and concept – onto the aether website in his Open Design Archives, encouraging feedback in order to help the ongoing project widen its perspective.

INDUCTION HOUSE – THE FISHING KIT

Architectural prototype
(the first two were 'The Fish Tank' and
'Distributed Projection Structure')
aether architecture (Adam Somlai-Fischer,
Péter Hudini, Anita Pozna, Bengt Sjölén)
Exhibited at the Kunsthalle Budapest, 2003
(prototype 1); Kiasma Centre for
Contemporary Art, Pixelache festival,
Helsinki, Finland, 2004 (prototype 2);
ISEA2004, Helsinki, Finland; and Gallery U,
Hungarian Cultural Institute, Helsinki

Somlai-Fischer sees that by dissolving the physical structure in 'the flux of interactive media, with media simultaneously becoming 'actual and spatial', the interaction created is 'symbolic, not really trying to function or process information, but to transform the physical entity in a non-physical way'. He applies the systems thinking of complexity science, producing several modes of concepts, each informing each other, back and forth, with the 'House' developing as a whole system without a predetermined hierarchy. This creates a stepping stone to a new relationship between technology and design, in which 'the role and effect of technology reveal a more profound relation between design and design tools and, in the process, as Flusser defined it, it becomes possible to "turn the automatic apparatus against automation."'

SOFT SPACE WITH PRESENCE

In the UK there are few, if any, institutions that support interactive spatial design outside academia. The Arts Council and the Science Museum have an active art programme involving artists and designers through the commissioning of their work. From 2006 the long-standing arts organisation The Public will open its new technologically mediated community art centre in West Bromwich (see page 104). FACT, the country's leading organization for the commissioning and presentation of film, video and new media art forms in Liverpool, seems wedded to film and digital video-based media for the moment.[40] In this climate of absence, practitioners make their own global institutional connections. In academia, the roles of the Architectural Association's Design Research Laboratory (DRL)[41] and the Bartlett School of Architecture – through its Interactive Architecture Workshop, and the Interaction Design Department of the Royal College of Art – over the last ten years have

SCENTS OF SPACE
Installation
Usman Haque, Josephine Pletts and Dr Luca Turin, 2002
Exhibited at the Bartlett School of Architecture, London, UK
2002

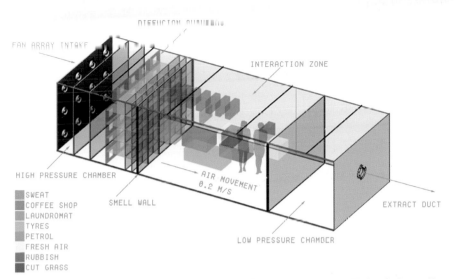

DIFFUSION CHAMBERS
FAN ARRAY INTAKE
INTERACTION ZONE
HIGH PRESSURE CHAMBER
SWEAT
COFFEE SHOP
LAUNDROMAT
TYRES
PETROL
FRESH AIR
RUBBISH
CUT GRASS
SMELL WALL
AIR MOVEMENT
0.2 M/S
EXTRACT DUCT
LOW PRESSURE CHAMBER

proved vital in providing a conceptual focus to design. Tobi Schneidler (born Munich, 1972; see page 106), an AA alumnus, is carving out an international course in the field; Jason Bruges and Usman Haque, both UK-based architects and products of the Bartlett, work as full-time consultants in this field, although Haque operates more like an artist because, up until now, he has developed project concepts and then secured funding from international bodies such as the Daniel Langlois Foundation for Art, Science and Technology in Toronto[42] and the Wellcome Trust, the world's largest medical research charity, based in London. Bruges relies less on grants and more on commercial commissions. Haque, who until 2005 taught at the Bartlett's Interactive Architecture Workshop, works with specialists (biophysicist Dr Luca Turin,[43] Professor Chris French, Head of Anomalistic Psychology at Goldsmiths College of Art in London[44] interaction and wearable computing designer Despina Papadopoulos[45] and architect Adam Somlai-Fischer, (see page 56) on specific projects, and was formerly the partner of architect Josephine Pletts, with whom he founded Pletts Haque, an architectural firm.

Haque specializes in interaction design and research, using conventional technology unconventionally to explore the ways people relate to each other and to their surrounding space. He works like an artist, mostly creating projects speculatively and then looking for funding. He designs physical environments and builds the software that brings them to life. His interactive and telecommunications works have been exhibited internationally, and with Pletts he was commissioned to design a global interactive tourist node by the Interaction Design Institute Ivrea in Italy, develop interactive elements for London bus shelters and research the spatial applications of smell for the Wellcome Trust, resulting in an installation, 'SCENTS OF SPACE' (2002). Now independent, Haque's projects investigate the phenomenological potential of architecture based on systems that combine hard space, such as walls, floors and ceilings, and soft space – arising from the sensuous, non-tangible elements present, such as sounds, smells, heat, colours and electromagnetic waves.

HIS PROJECTS INVESTIGATE THE PHENOMENOLOGICAL POTENTIAL OF ARCHITECTURE BASED ON SYSTEMS THAT COMBINE HARD SPACE, SUCH AS WALLS, FLOORS AND CEILINGS, AND SOFT SPACE.

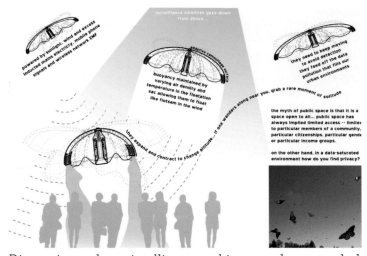

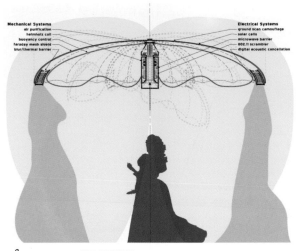

FLOATABLES
Floating interactive vessels
Haque Design + Research (Usman Haque)
2004

Discussions about intelligent architecture have tended to focus on environmental controls such as sun louvres, centralized ICT systems or retro-reflective surfaces, but new technologies now permit us to have a conversation with our environments. Haque believes further advances will allow the designed environment to go beyond being perceived as a certain category of 'interface' and evolve instead into a spatial 'operating system'. Users will have unprecedented potential to create personal programs and explore their own systems of social intercourse. Haque's own projects are investigative, going beyond the pragmatic to using technology in a playful, novel way to build a deeper sense of spatial potential. He draws on techniques used by media artists, and has been heavily influenced by cybernetician Gordon Pask, as well as being inspired by the Cybernetic Serendipity exhibition held at the ICA in 1968.

While 'Scents of Space' created an interactive, reconfigurable spatial 'smell collage' using everything from fragrance to the noxious contents of the dustbin, 'Haunt', an experimental chamber first created in a private house in north London in 2005, works with humidity, temperatures and electromagnetic and sonic frequencies to achieve a very different aim: designing a space that appears to be haunted. He uses infrasound (a multi-channel sound system with woofer speakers, which operates below the threshold of sound), an air-control system that creates slow, moving streams of air to give the impression of invisible movement and a variable radio-frequency generator to make undulating electromagnetic spaces. Visually, nothing moves except the constant subtle breath of the 'air con' system, but by varying the contrasts of colours and light levels and creating other optical illusions, Haque provokes unsettling visual phenomena. He does not try to debunk popular notions of the paranormal, but to show 'how the perceptions of space and objects in space are intricately affected by things we are not immediately conscious of'.

HAQUE SHOWS 'HOW THE PERCEPTIONS OF SPACE AND OBJECTS IN SPACE ARE INTRICATELY AFFECTED BY THINGS WE ARE NOT IMMEDIATELY CONSCIOUS OF.'

SKY EAR
Interactive electromagnetic cloud
Haque Design + Research (Usman Haque),
2003–4
Electronic engineer: Senseinate Inc.
Structural engineer: Fluid Structures
Exhibited at the Belluard Bollwerk
International Festival, Fribourg, Switzerland;
VIPER, Basel, Switzerland; and at the
National Maritime Museum, Greenwich,
London, UK
2004
Photos: Ai Hasegawa (above),
David Rothschild (right)

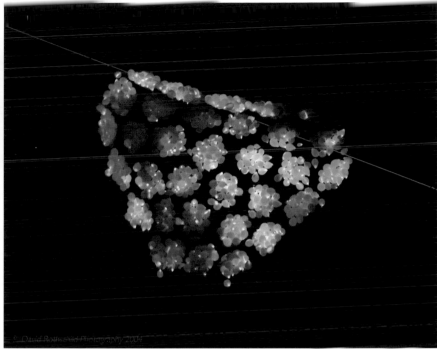

Electromagnetic waves in the ether combined with mobile phones produced the interactive element of the '**SKY EAR**' project (launched at the Belluard Bollwerk International Festival, Fribourg, Switzerland and the National Maritime Museum, Greenwich, London, in 2004). Haque is interested in how mobile phones condition our use of space now that they have become ubiquitous. Furthermore, because most people enjoy using them it is a good way to get a bigger audience involved. The project itself centred physically on a non-rigid 'cloud' made up of hundreds of glowing helium balloons. From it were suspended mobile phones, brightly coloured LEDs and electromagnetic sensors emitting different-coloured lights when activated. These miniature sensor circuits (simple gaussmeters) detected levels of electromagnetic radiation at a variety of frequencies. When they were activated the sensor circuits caused the LEDs to illuminate. 'When an audience member uses a phone during the cloud flight, they are not using it just as a remote control device: the cloud is actually responding to the electromagnetic fields created by the phones in the cloud,' said Haque.

Released from its ground moorings, the cloud slowly floated up into the sky, its balloons enclosed in a carbon-fibre and net structure 25 metres in diameter tethered to the ground by six cables. Once fully risen, it was held aloft at a height of 60 metres, and in Greenwich climbed to a height of over 100 metres, watched by over 3,500 people. Passing through varying radio and microwave spaces as it rose, it appeared 'like a glowing jellyfish sampling the electromagnetic spectrum rather like a vertical radar sweep', said Haque. Spectators on the ground used their phones to call into the cloud to listen to the distant electromagnetic sounds of the sky, and as they did so, their calls changed the internal electromagnetic topography inside the cloud, and altered the glow and colour intensity of part of the balloon cloud.

The balloons acted as diffusers for the six ultra-bright LED lights that mixed with millions of colours controlled by the individual sensors inside each balloon. They could communicate with each other via infrared, creating patterns across the surface of the cloud. Feedback within the sensor network created ripples of light similar to rumbling thunder and flashes of lightning. At the Greenwich event, spectators and also people on the Web were able to dial up the cloud using freephone numbers and manipulate the patterns of illumination. 'Sky Ear' received funding from the Daniel Langlois Foundation for Art, Science and Technology, enabling Haque's most ambitious project to date.

'Electromagnetic waves exist just about everywhere in our atmosphere,' said Haque. 'The cloud will show both how a natural invisible electromagnetism pervades our environment and how our mobile phone calls and text messages delicately affect the new and existing electromagnetic fields.' These waves have long existed as natural phenomena – distant storms, radio waves emanating from stars, gamma rays from elements here on earth or even electrical waves inside our own skulls. More recently, human beings have begun contributing to the situation with mobile phones, pagers, medical devices and television broadcasts, with mobiles and power lines giving cause for alarm about the health effects of electromagnetic radiation.

'Sky Ear' engages us in the reality that electromagnetic space – also defined as hertzian space by the designer Tony Dunne (of Dunne + Raby) in his groundbreaking book of the same name, 'Herzian Tales' – is physical and non-virtual, and all electronic objects are a form of radio, leaking radiation into space.[46] The balloons, being more than just detectors, function as cellular automata, and Haque envisages creating larger patterns, with them all talking to each other. 'Sky Ear' is groundbreaking because it breaks the perceptual boundaries between the physical and virtual by encouraging people to become creative participants in a hertzian performance, allowing us to see our daily interactions with the invisible topographies of electromagnetic space.

The gripping feeling that 'something is out there', that a space might be haunted, is another topic Haque has investigated, again through public involvement. Working from the idea that a phantom is a constructed being, he created 'HAUNT', a tent-like space in the room of a private house, out of dexion and fabric pinned together with bulldog clips, reached through a corridor-like buffer zone to dull the senses. Here he set up a variable radio-frequency generator emitting electromagnetic waves taken from two haunted houses through two coils in the wall and a multi-

THE CLOUD WILL SHOW BOTH HOW A NATURAL INVISIBLE ELECTROMAGNETISM PERVADES OUR ENVIRONMENT AND HOW OUR MOBILE PHONE CALLS AND TEXT MESSAGES DELICATELY AFFECT THE NEW AND EXISTING ELECTROMAGNETIC FIELDS.
USMAN HAQUE

HAUNT
Experimental chamber
Haque Design + Research (Usman Haque),
2005
Installed at a private house,
Finsbury Park, London, UK
2005

channel sound system, creating a subsonic infrasound topography, one on either side of the room. The combined effect elicited sporadically the sensation of presence. An air-control system used earlier in the 'Scents of Space' was activated to position areas of humidity, dryness and cool air. In the first prototype presented, visitors had a galvanic skin-response meter strapped to their arms before entering the space to track their levels of arousal. Haque believes that beyond infrasound, humidity, temperature, air movement and electromagnetism, other factors affect the perception of hauntings: the psychology of the individuals, the desire to believe something is happening (also observed when people encounter simulated intelligence systems) and the social environment in which the hauntings are observed. A responsive work like 'Haunt' taps into the fluid thresholds between all these factors, internal and external.

Haque makes a distinction between reactive and interactive environments. 'Reactive implies a one-way causal relationship; interactivity, a circularity of cause and effect, an iterative relationship.' His clear preference is for environments that are themselves interactors, because they imply reciprocity and an equality of transactions, with creative outputs. He awaits an interactive environment that is simply intelligent, as opposed to 'amenable and intelligent'.

SENSOR PARK
Installation, one of a number of artworks
created as part of 'Edge Town'
Shona Kitchen and Ben Hooker, 2002
Exhibited during the 9th Venice Architecture
Biennale, Italy
2004

TECHNOLOGICALLY MEDIATED ECOLOGIES

The harnessing of invisible environmental phenomena in 'Sky Ear'
can be seen in the work of the UK-based architect Shona Kitchen
(born St Andrews, Scotland, 1968), who has developed a career as a
multi-disciplinary designer. The imaginary '**EDGE TOWN**', a design-led
research project part funded by IBM she has evolved with Ben Hooker
(born Bath, UK, 1974), who also trained in interactive design at the Royal
College of Art, considers future living in urban environments with an
ever-increasing electronic component. Its electro-physical topography is
defined by a number of design propositions for housing, employing
'noise farmers', an interactive ecosystem of interactive objects and
'sensor parks', areas of fenced off land with an array of monitoring and
display systems responding to the electro-physical flux of the environment. 'We are using the reality that contemporary environments are
dense with data and pollution. Living with the consequences can be
made into something positive,' says Kitchen. The noise farmers are
utilitarian-looking devices stemming from the question: if natural environments thrive on sunlight, what does a technological environment
thrive on? What is a man-made, synthetic ecology? They thrive on data,
with the Solenoid hedge opening its leaves dramatically following
a surge in data flow, like a dandelion releasing its seeds. One of 'Edge
Town's group of installations, the **CELLULAR NOISE MAKER**, a box like a large
portable radio, stores data which is shown as an intricate pattern on
a vacuum-fluorescent display and later becomes a score to generate
sounds.

WE ARE USING
THE REALITY THAT
CONTEMPORARY
ENVIRONMENTS
ARE DENSE
WITH DATA AND
POLLUTION.
LIVING WITH THE
CONSEQUENCES
CAN BE MADE
INTO SOMETHING
POSITIVE.
SHONA KITCHEN

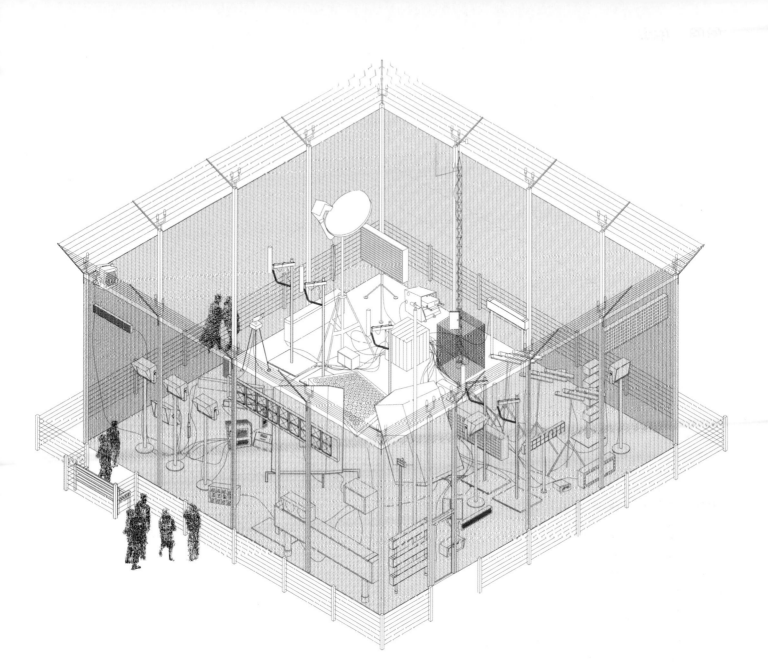

Like Haque, Swiss architects Décosterd + Rahm (Philippe Rahm, born Pully, Switzerland, 1967 and Jean-Gilles Décosterd, born Lausanne, Switzerland, 1963, now working independently) have explored the unstable impact of environments on our metabolism, sensory states of being and perception of our temporality. They want to understand better our relationship between the material world, of which architecture is a part with its specific constructions, and our ambient environment, and do this by creating prototype and demonstration spaces, as well as modifying control of water, light and air. By bringing about a physiological distortion and expression through biotechnological means, affecting temperature, humidity and light, they provoke reactions and confrontations by the body.

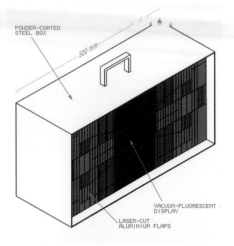

POWDER-COATED
STEEL BOX

500 mm

VACUUM-FLUORESCENT
DISPLAY

LASER-CUT
ALUMINIUM FLAPS

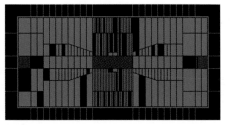

CELLULAR NOISE MAKER
Installation, one of a number of artworks
created as part of 'Edge Town', an interactive
design research project, proposals and
installation
Shona Kitchen and Ben Hooker, 2002
Exhibited during the 9th Venice Architecture
Biennale, Italy
2004

Most of their installations to date have not been about form, size, colour
or representation, like typical architecture, but about enlarging a sense of
sensory information – or making, for their own means, a conscious lack
of it, in the case of '**HORMONIUM**'. Created for the Swiss pavilion at the 2002
Venice Architecture Biennale, it had a Plexiglas floor with fluorescent
UV tubes; the oxygen level was reduced to 14°C, inducing a form of
euphoria not unlike that produced by an alpine climate, in a degeogra-
phized environment. The '**HYDRACAFÉ**' (a new café for l'Ecole Nationale
Supérieure des Beaux-Arts de Paris, 2004), created with artist Jean-Luc
Vilmouth, has a dual form of rehydration in that it is not just a place for
drinking, but a humidified environment too, and counters an economical-
ly and geographically specific public spaces' norm for 'full-on' air conditioning. With a trough of water installed on the roof and ultrasonics on the
ground, the environment is made capable of generating drier and wetter
zones. The '**MELATONIN ROOM**' (2001) tries to find a relationship between the
body and space.[47] It too has two manufactured climates, this time
produced in alternation. Electro-magnetic rays suppress the body's
production of melatonin, causing the room to become a physically
motivating, chemically exciting place. The second climate is produced
by the diffusion of ultraviolet rays that promote the production of
melatonin, and therefore create sleepiness in the people in the space.

HYDRACAFF

Cafeteria Interior, L'École Nationale
Supérieur des Beaux-Arts de Paris, France
Décosterd + Rahm (Philippe Rahm and
Jean-Gilles Décosterd) with Jean-Luc
Vilmouth, 2004
Client: Commande du CNAP (Centre national
des arts plastiques, Ministère de la culture),
ENSBA (Ecole National Supérieure des
Beaux-Arts de Paris)
Photo: © Décosterd + Rahm

HORMONIUM

Installation
Décosterd + Rahm (Philippe Rahm and
Jean-Gilles Décosterd), 2002
Exhibited Swiss Pavilion, 8th Biennale
of Architecture, Venice
2002
Photo: Jean-Michel Landecy

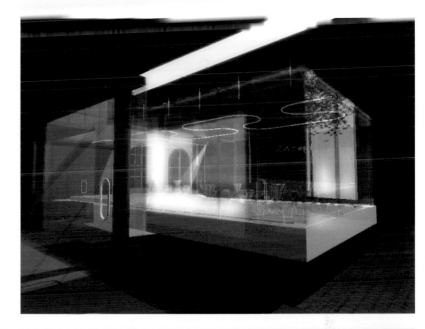

MELATONIN ROOM
Installation
Decosterd + Rahm (Philippe Rahm and
Jean-Gilles Décosterd)
SFMOMA/San Francisco Museum of
Modern Art, USA
2001

The architects' project entitled '**LUCY MACKINTOSH CONTEMPORARY ART GALLERY**' (2004), a thermic installation with a desk, library and exhibition space, has different heating levels throughout the space – in the seated area, 21°C; gallery, 16°C; archives, 12°C – created by a tubular network of warm and cold water, and a convection air system. Temperature levels are 12–21°C in winter and 18–30°C in summer, accommodating the fact that when one walks, one does not need the same temperature as for sitting. The ultraviolet light in '**GHOST FLAT**' (2004) is also graduated along the electromagnetic spectrum: the bathroom is green, the bedroom blue and the living room red. The intention is to give a sense of dual location, and of intersecting spectrums of spaces haunting each other like ghosts. 'It's important to be aware that space changes, and is not a void but full of things, wavelengths, for instance, so our relationship with space is not superficial,' says Rahm. He cites the science-fiction works of nineteenth-century writers like Jules Verne, who evoked artificial 'parellel world' spaces, and technological advances like street lights, which caused a 'revolution of the astronomical rhythm of the world'. Their 'endrocrine architecture, to be breathed', makes us aware of the 'normalization of the climate' we experience as a result of the artificial consistency brought about by modernity.

IT'S IMPORTANT TO BE AWARE THAT SPACE CHANGES, AND IS NOT A VOID BUT FULL OF THINGS, WAVELENGTHS, FOR INSTANCE, SO OUR RELATIONSHIP WITH SPACE IS NOT SUPERFICIAL.
PHILIPPE RAHM

LUCY MACKINTOSH CONTEMPORARY ART GALLERY
Installation
Philippe Rahm with Jean-Gilles Décosterd,
2004
Client: Lucy Mackintosh and Cyril Veillon
Galerie d'art contemporain, Lausanne,
Switzerland
2004

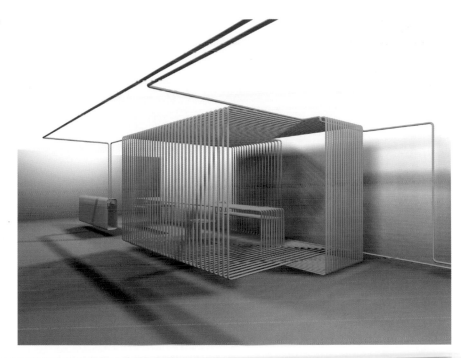

GHOST FLAT
Installation
Philippe Rahm
CCA Kitakyushu, Japan
2004
Photo: © Philippe Rahm

PHYSICAL-VIRTUAL COMMUNICATION

Conducting your love life or expressing your innermost feelings through an architectural medium is a pretty far-reaching social proposition. '**D-TOWER**', a collaboration between architect Lars Spuybroek of NOX in Rotterdam and Q.S. Serafijn, a Rotterdam-based artist, aims to do just that. One evening in 2004 in the city of Doetinchem, in the east of the Netherlands, in front of a huge crowd, 'D-Tower' was opened, a zoomorphic-looking permanent public tower. Simultaneously, a website was launched with responses to questions created by Serafijn, expressing the intensities of participants' feelings of love, hate, happiness and fear evoked in the process.[48] The tower converted the emotions of these answers into colour, transmitting 'the state of the town' every evening – the colour of the most intensely felt emotion. After running for a month, the architects concluded that it had often been blue (for happiness) or red (for love), and sometimes green (for hate), but not yellow (for fear). Each six months a different group of 50 inhabitants will complete further editions of the questionnaire, becoming more precise, and with all the answers translated into the form of different 'landscapes' shown on the website. Spuybroek explains that in the process, all the ins and outs of their emotional lives are made visible, including ongoing discussions about hot issues. People responded to an initial newspaper advertisement via the website for 50 participants and were selected according to age, sex and neighbourhood.

D-TOWER
Installation and website
Lars Spuybroek/NOX, Q.S. Serafijn
and the V2_Lab
Doetinchem, the Netherlands
Comissioned by the city of Doetinchem
2004

At night the light of the tall, prefabricated epoxy structure goes on simultaneously with the street lights, and onlookers can also check its colour on a webcam. 'D-Tower is a coherent hybrid of different media, where architecture is part of a larger interactive system of relationships,' says Spuybroek. In the capsule placed underneath the tower, inhabitants of the city can place their personal messages concerning the 'landscapes' shown on the site. Creating a connection between all these elements, the tower also triggers the sending of pre-prepared love letters and flowers from and to designated addresses. At the end of each year it will present a prize of 10,000 Euros to the address in the city that scores the highest level of emotions according to the result of the website computing.

T-GARDEN ENVIRONMENT
Performance/play space installation
Sponge (Sha Xin Wei, Chris Salter,
Laura Farabo) and FoAM (Maja Kuzmanovic,
Evelina Kusaite, Nik Gaffney, Steven Pickles,
Dave Tonessen)
First prototype shown at SIGGRAPH,
New Orleans, 2000
Second prototype installed at the Ars
Electronica Festival, Linz, Austria, 2001
Fuller scale prototype shown at Las Palmas
by V2, Rotterdam, the Netherlands, as part
of V2's European Cultural Capital, 2003,
and other European, North American and
Australian settings, 2003–

PLAY AND PERFORMANCE

'D-Tower' uses technology to make a responsive environment for citizens not just based on Web interaction, but allied to changing physical states in an urban context. The role of the Dutch body V2 Institute for the Unstable Media, has clearly fostered greater public awareness of their importance, encouraging in 2005 the leading telecommunications firm KPN to commission a German artist, Tim Otto Roth (born 1974), to design Pixelsex, an interactive light work for its headquarters building overlooking the River Maas.[49] Many projects are first set up behind the scenes as cumulative prototypes within a framework of ongoing research. The **'T-GARDEN'** environment designed by San Francisco-based association Sponge[50] and the Belgian/Dutch group FoAM is a leading example of the hybrid play/performance genre. 'T-Garden's' 'performers' comprise several visitors within a specified time cycle, who together 'shape' media based on their movement and that of those around them. On entry, they are invited to put on clothing designed with various physical and material constraints. Sensors are embedded in the clothing[51] – accelerometers measuring the degree of acceleration, tilt and gravity of each person's movement, as well as wireless/wearable clothing – so that it interferes with their usual ways of relating to the world. This intimate, on-the-body computing allows data collected to be sent via wireless Ethernet to a central logic system, which analyses what is happening overall in the 'T-Garden', and then sends commands to the sound and computer graphics systems based on these analyses.

'T-Garden' is immersive, and evolutionary in the sense that its media system is designed with a high level of real-time physical responsiveness, tangibility and media choreographic potential. The visitors experience an immediate engagement with the room's media, and see visible traces of their new gestures and movements as particles. Because floor movement is directly coupled to sound, they quickly realize their bodily effort and movement is needed to add their voices to the mix of sounds in the room. Through time, the room's interaction and media complexity increases as players evolve from novice to more advanced levels.

Initially basic gestures and sound ideas were explored with two people at a time; later, higher level languages of mathematics and computer science were introduced. After the second phase was presented,[52] a fuller scale work was shown in Rotterdam, with more participants and more complex interaction scenarios, before phase three was launched and tested in various international settings. 'T-Garden' is important as a prototype of a new open-source model of inter disciplinary collaboration. With each stage, tests have enlarged the team's understanding of social studies of technology, experimental phenomenology, topological media, wireless sensing, wearable computing and responsive dynamic media systems.

ANTHROPOMORPHIC ENVIRONMENTS

One feature of play-based responsive environments is the anthropomorphizing of objects or spaces. An early work of Usman Haque, '**MOODY MUSHROOM FLOOR**' (1996), developed moods and aspirations in response to the ways in which people react to it. Each one of the group of eight mushrooms – small structures with lights underneath them – positioned in a room experimented with how successful they might be in adopting different moods, randomly becoming sullen, alluring or capricious, for instance, to see whether they could achieve what they wanted when they were in that mood. If a mushroom tried to be sullen, for example, it would try to keep people away from it while learning its goals through trial and error, specifically which patterns of light, smell and sound work best at repelling people. If it discovered that it was successful at it, it would tend to be more sullen in the future.

After a while, visitors experienced pleasant conditions in areas of the space – comforting light patterns, good smells, soothing sounds – but also other areas with just the opposite, with disturbing light patterns, bad smells and harsh sounds. However, the trigger for their orientation was how the people collectively responded to their environmental conditions in the first place. The project was loosely a prototype for 'Haunt', described earlier, with its range of outputs. It is striking that Haque used the work as a medium for wayward qualities and their 'perfection', rather than their restriction, but then his work is consistently based on anomalistic models.

MOODY MUSHROOM FLOOR
Installation
1. Network and output coordination,
2. Sensory outputs
Usman Haque, 1996
Installed at the Bartlett School of
Architecture, London, UK
1996

CONCEPTUAL GAMES

Sometimes common perceptions of interactive works for a number of participants veer towards thinking of them as a kind of video game when they are not. A recent work shown in Paris at the 2004 Villette-Numerique Festival for art and technology, '**CHRONOPOLIS**', by Chris Salter (born Beaumont, Texas, USA, 1967) and graphic designer Erik Adigard with Mathew Biederman and Gregory Cowley, was a 15 x 15-metre inhabitable projection which the public walked over. A giant projected clock, it kept changing its timekeeping based on the density of crowds gathering in the space. Apparently some people expected the typical video-game experience, where they would get an instant response to their actions. What in fact happened was that once the population on the floor reached capacity, the image and the soundscape morphed into the world of 'Chronopolis' time. While 'normal' time had been represented by a chaotic overlay or multiple time grids and a jarring noise, as the structure moved towards 'Chronopolis' time, the scene simplified and gained order, shown as a clean 10 x 10-metre grid and serene music.

CHRONOPOLIS
Installation
2004
Chris Salter, Erik Adigard/M.A.D with
Mathew Biederman and Gregory Cowley
Installed at the 2004 Villette-Numérique
Festival for art and technology, Paris, France

Installations of this kind often aim to encourage participants to experience a parallel reality of the world. The '**HIDDEN WORLDS OF NOISE AND VOICE**' (2002), an interactive audiovisual installation, allows up to six participants to 'see' each other's voices made visible in the form of coloured, animated graphic figurations that appear to emerge from their mouths when they speak. The shapes relate to the unique qualities of the vocalist's volume, pitch and timbre. To bring about this 'extrasensory perception', they wear special see-through data glasses that register and superimpose 3-D graphics into the real world. The installation was created by artist and composer Golan Levin (born 1972) and Zachary Lieberman in collaboration with the Ars Electronica Futurelab through its Artist in Residence Programme. More than just about surprising each other with silly noises, the views captured through the augmented reality eyepieces show the way in which these forms are superimposed onto physical reality. Levin's work brings whimsicality and provocation to the task of unveiling a parallel reality. His concert '**DIALTONES**' (2001) was wholly performed by the carefully choreographed dialling and ringing of the audience's own mobile phones. A graduate of MIT Media Laboratory, in between degrees he worked simultaneously as an interaction designer and research scientist at Interval Research.

DIALTONES
Concert with mobile phones
Golan Levin with Scott Gibbons and Gregory Shakar, 2001
Brucknerhaus Auditorium, as part of Ars Electronica Festival, Linz, Austria, 2001; and at Artplage Mobile de Jura as a production of the Swiss National Exhibition, 2002

LIGHT DOME
Christmas 'lighting landscape'
Veronika Valk, Winy Maas/MVRDV
and Rogier van der Heide/Arup
Tallinn, Estonia
2004

OPTING OUT OF DIGITAL MEDIA

It is healthy that the involvement of a digital element in an interactive art solution that is designed to be used by a number of people at one time is questioned, and many contexts make it either unnecessary or unaffordable; that does not mean their mechanical character is less effective. Veronika Valk (born Tallinn, Estonia, 1976), an Estonian architect who runs Zizi & Yoyo, an architectural practice in Estonia (along with her other studio, Kavakava), maintains that local 'conditions have made me believe more in actual physical interaction than a digital one. When aiming for playfulness I try to avoid remote controls or sensors – it never works technically up here, or doesn't last, because public authorities lack the funds to keep digital interactive installations running properly.' So when she brought in Winy Maas from MVRDV and Rogier van der Heide, the lighting designer, from Arup, to collaborate with Zizi & Yoyo on new Christmas street lighting in the historic district of Tallinn, they came up with the idea for a '**LIGHT DOME**' over Tallinn. A huge number of white, helium-filled balloons tethered to the ground by white sugar bags that served as seats bobbed about in a smoke cloud, illuminated by sports lighting. From here 50–250 people could 'choreograph' the balloon cloud, creating the sense of an interactive 'lighting landscape'.

LIGHT DOME
Christmas 'lighting landscape'
Veronika Valk, Winy Maas/MVRDV
and Rogier van der Heide/Arup
Tallinn, Estonia
2004

JAPAN'S INTERACTIVE COMMUNICATION EXPERIENCE

Spatial interactive works have been 'harvested' in a number of corporate headquarters, especially in Japan, for instance in corridor spaces of the Dentsu advertising agency building in Tokyo, designed by Jean Nouvel, whose fast and fully glazed elevators with flashing red and blue lights swooshing people up high over the city's heterotopic landscape make it pretty interactive in its own right. The world-famous financial news agency Bloomberg's London office has featured projects by the Light Surgeons, but since late 2002 the firm's high-rise headquarters in Tokyo's Marunouchi have featured an installation in a dedicated space on the ground floor. Visible from the street, '**ICE**', which stands for interactive communicative experience, is a 'smart' info-lounge planted within this busy urban space, designed by architects Klein Dytham[53] with Toshio Iwai (born Kira-town, Aichi prefecture, Japan, 1962), a leading Japanese interactive designer. It permits people – staff and visitors – to process and play with data in a very tangible and experiential way. The duo wanted to create something unique and playful that had never before existed in this working environment, but rejected the idea of either a cyber café or an inevitably more isolated gallery space. The installation is a 5 x 3.5-metre glass wall suspended from the ceiling like a large stalactite or icicle. It is also quite deep – 10 centimetres – in order to be earthquake proof. FTSE and NASDAQ financial data are lightly visible close up, represented as electronic ticker tape. If the stock is up, the stock sign swells; if it drops, the sign shrinks below the line like digital shadows that rise and fall.

ICE
Permanent installation
Klein Dytham with Toshio Iwai
Bloomberg headquarters, Tokyo, Japan
Commissioned by Bloomberg, Tokyo
2001
Photo: Katsuhisa Kida

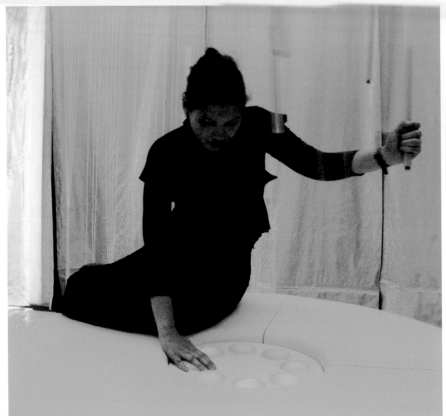

TUNE ME
Immersive conceptual radio
Interaction Design Institute Ivrea
Exhibited at Touch Me: design and sensation,
Victoria & Albert Museum, London, UK,
2005
Photo: Stefano Mirti

Infrared sensors behind the surface detect visitors' presence from 500 millimetres away – they do not need to touch it – and the data begins to interact with their bodily movements, the columns of numbers starting to fluctuate. A menu scrolls down the screen, giving the visitor four digital play options – a harp, shadow, wave or volley ball. Glowing, bifurcating coloured light forms like tree branches instantly represent the sounds of music. The sensors convert movements and touch into optical and acoustic signals, and these inputs are relayed back as vibrant, ever-changing reflective patterns, like manipulable fire, which cast giant electronic shadows. KDa is already well known for its electronic billboards and 3-D hoardings-cum-architecture, but 'ICE' is one of their first stabs at making an interactive game spatial. With its engaging interface, elegantly installed, 'ICE' promotes the personalization of space by reacting in real time to the body as a biofeedback mechanism. The wall is constantly processing information received virtually and physical information about human presence, and converting the input it receives from the large number of electronic sensors behind the screen.

'ICE' is designed to last for four to five years and clearly constitutes a new environmental genre, an alternative on-premises amusement arcade, one that has already proved very popular. An innocent yet knowing design, it merges perceptual boundaries between office interior and street, work and play, data and body.

LEARNING THROUGH PLAY

Elsewhere the Interaction Institute in Italy, an independent, non-profit technological research institute established by Telecom Italian and Olivetti in 2001, has produced many exemplary prototypes engaging with play and leisure. With '**CICCIO FLIES OVER TUSCANY**', an interactive inflatable designed by architect and Ivrea Professor Stefano Mirti[54] and students Daniele Mancini and Francesca Sassaroli, children entered the spaces and found a table with 30 objects. Each one came from a different part of Tuscany, and was embedded with an RFID tag. When a child chose his object and placed it in a special part of the table, a projection of an aerial 3-D map would begin, transforming the whole inflatable. The projections made its light blue fabric constantly change its skin; the playfulness of the concept kept children engaged, and the geographers happy that some of their discipline's knowledge was being imparted in the process. Mirti, who works with computer scientist Walter Aprile, applies an ethos of 'learning by doing' to the evolution of processes and tools to achieve narrative goals: 'A mediatheque, a reactive façade, tells and embodies stories, and these stories are our business.'[55]

A MEDIATHEQUE, A REACTIVE FACADE, TELLS AND EMBODIES STORIES, AND THESE STORIES ARE OUR BUSINESS.
STEFANO MIRTI

CICCIO FLIES OVER TUSCANY
Installation prototype
Interaction Design Institute Ivrea, Italy
(Daniele Mancini, Francesca Sassaroli)
Commission by the Geographical Society
of Tuscany
2004

INTELLIGENT WALLS AND FLOORS

AN INTELLIGENT WALL IS, AT ITS SIMPLEST, AN ENVIRONMENTAL MANIFESTATION OF TECHNOLOGY ALREADY BEING USED.

An intelligent wall is, at its simplest, an environmental manifestation of technology already being used. In the public contexts of office foyers, airports and covered retail spaces used every day there is currently little flexibility for experiments involving the viewer, and vertical surfaces in the city, being a form of real estate in themselves, are dominated by commercial imagery. At the micro-scale in working spaces and specific cultural contexts, this is changing.

Stefano Mirti and artist and designer Crispin Jones's[56] '**HUMAN SCREEN PROPOSAL**' for the Interaction Institute Ivrea in 2004[57] was not executed, but it is a good model of an interactive wall as a visitor attractor on an architectural scale. Different modes included images of visitors captured using cameras and prepared images; visitors could be invited to submit comments by SMS, or simply play with the displays directly, making text or just doodling.

FLOCK WALLPAPER
Interactive wall
Jason Bruges
Architect of foyer and bedroom suites:
Kathryn Findlay
Hotel Puerta América, Madrid, Spain
Commissioned by Grupo Urvasco
2005

HUMAN SCREEN PROPOSAL
Interactive screen concept for a public space
Interaction Institute Ivrea (Stefano Mirti and
Crispin Jones)
Design project for the Salone Del Mobile,
Milan, 2004 (not realized)

Bland meeting rooms have been accused of dampening creativity. Jason Bruges's '**ART WALL**', an interactive artwork for the boardroom of Five, the television channel based in London's Covent Garden, uses interactive media in a way that is fresh, unclunky and easily adjustable. A set of LED panels embedded in the lining of the room, it is controlled by central computer and programmed to display artwork, including Five's own live feed, creating different moods to suit a variety of situations in a room used for everything from meetings to theatre-style presentations.

THE SPACE BECOMES AS EASY TO CHANGE AS AN IMAGE, AND THE IMAGE BECOMES MORE IMMERSIVE.

NAZIHA MESTAOUI (ELECTRONIC SHADOW)

Other types of smart surface respond to the human voice or music. The dynamics of Dutch architect Daan Roosegaarde's '**4D PIXEL**' moving wall result from these, magnet technology and intelligent software, and can even write letters. It is made of hundreds of physical pixels that activate in response to stimuli, to display patterns or text. A graduate of the Berlage Institute in Rotterdam, Roosegaarde (born Nieuwkoop, the Netherlands, 1979) is developing the project on a larger scale as a public building facade.

HeHe's '**BRIX**', a wall of virtual bricks designed during a three-month research residency at the Interaction Design Institute Ivrea, also explores new ways of structuring information within architecture, injecting a sense of performance. With a human hand, they will transform themselves. When the lens of a camera mounted in front of the wall is touched, the surface of the wall reflects the image captured by the camera, in as many rectangular pixels. The image of the 'inter-actor' slips onto the wall and after a few seconds, freezes as a photograph. The first prototypes developed simple behaviours that worked with light. Each unit mounted with sensors responded to touch, and would slowly light up or dim itself, depending on its previous state and the way it was touched, stimulating the experience of drawing with light, creating patterns and letters. This allows for direct interaction between individuals, so that two people separated by a wall can touch each other through light. 'Light Brix' was made up in an edition of 220 back-lit hexagonal 'pixels' and is now being developed for manufacture.

ART WALL
Interactive artwork
Jason Bruges
Boardroom of Five television channel,
London, UK
2005

SMARTSLAB
Multimedia display
Tom Barker/b consultants
Manufactured by SmartSlab™
2002

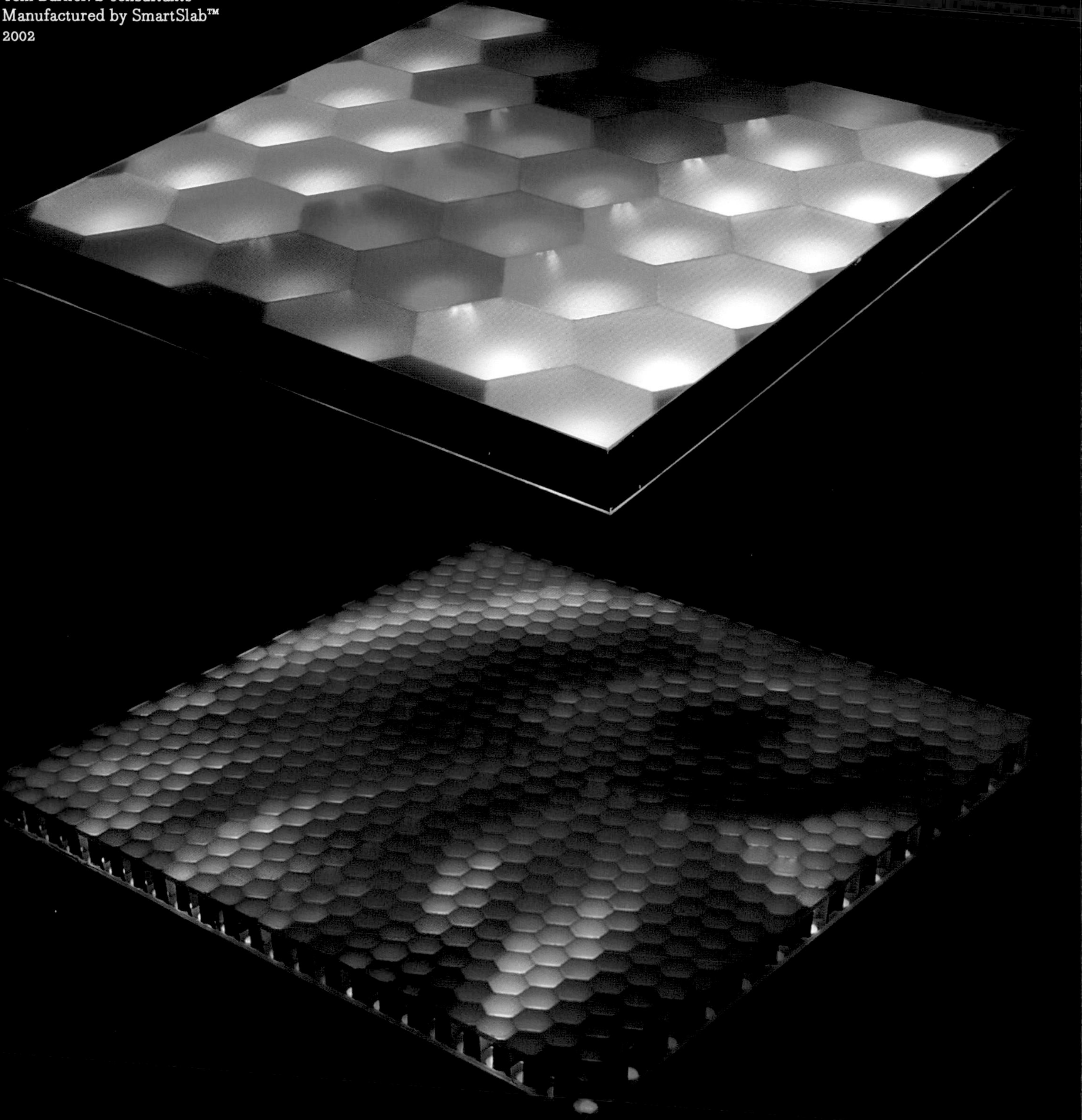

4D PIXEL

Daan Roosegaarde with Peter de Man, 2004
Electronics: KITT Engineering
Exhibited at the Berlage Institute, Rotterdam
2004

BRIX
Installation
HeHe (Helen Evans and Heiko Hansen)
Produced during Research Fellowship at
Interaction Design Institute Ivrea, Italy, 2001
Exhibited in 'HeHe', Mains d'Œuvres, St Ouen,
France, 2003; and in 'Invisibile', Centre for
Contemporary Art, Palazzo delle Papesse,
Siena, Italy
2004–5

'SMARTSLAB', a modular interactive system for diverse uses in the urban digital environment, not yet widely implemented, has also attracted a lot of attention. A multimedia display system based on an extremely tough, 60 square centimetre, 7.5 centimetre-deep modular structural tile, it was developed by Box Consultants (Tom Barker, principal of b consultants, born 1966, London), a design engineer responsible for over 14 years for many multi-disciplinary projects in the fields of industrial design, engineering, technology and architecture (and professor and head of the department of industrial design engineering at the Royal College of Art since 2004) and Jason Bruges. 'SmartSlab' is an arrangement of big hexagonal pixels in a honeycomb pattern, which can be combined to create small installations or huge display walls. The product attracted the early interest of London Underground, which may use it for dynamic signage. Richard Rogers Partnership is considering it for Heathrow's Terminal 5 and their Barcelona Bullring project, and potentially also for ceiling tiles with 'motion-tracking' sensors to detect the movement of people below. Inspired by the naturally efficient optics of a fly's eye, the pixels enable a finer image quality than that of a standard square. Inside, the light-emitting diode is capable of 16 million possible colours, and moving and still images on the display are controlled by a standard PC system using custom 'SmartSlab' software.

Direct Internet feeds with customized content can also be made available for tagged[58] or subscribed viewers, as well as a 'finger painting' mode to allow people to 'draw' or 'graffiti' on the panels. Also, viewer dwell-time recording for commercial purposes through proximity detectors can be part of the options, giving the pixel structures a potential surveillance aspect.

SmartSlab's potential as 'outdoor media' can be harnessed once Barker has further researched its creative applications. An American project evolved by the Responsive Environments Group at MIT Media Lab, 'The Magic Carpet' (2001, installed as 'The Stomping Ground' in the MIT Museum, 2002). This was an immersive, sensing space, with radars capturing upper body movement and the floor itself. The Group even designed several ambient soundscapes for the project, installing the systems in their office's lift lobbies. Passers-by stopped for extended periods to explore the sonic mappings. It was made up of a 1.8 x 3-metre sensor floor on top of a matrix of pressure-sensitive piezoelectric wires. These measured the position and intensity of footsteps, while radars sensed upper body motion, and a ranging sonar system monitored remote distance to people and objects.

H2O
Installation
Electronic Shadow (Naziha Mestaoui and Yacine Ait Kaci), 2004
Music: Stephan Haeri
Installed in the Boffi furniture showrooms in Paris, France, 2004; and in Milan during the Salone dei Mobile, Italy
2005

WARM AND COLD
Installation
Electronic Shadow
(Naziha Mestaoui and Yacine Ait Kaci)
Installed in the Cassina furniture showroom,
Paris, France, 2004–5

While such a project has yet to grace Wal-Mart or the average office reception, increasing numbers of corporate commissions for unique, possibly even poetic interfaces that are not about tag tracking or surveillance are being made for working or retail environments. They can capitalize on the growing convergence between new sensing modalities through the application of enabling technologies. Electronic Shadow, a studio established in Paris in 2000 by Naziha Mestaoui, a Brussels-born architect (1975), and Yacine Ait Kaci (born Paris, 1973), a graphic and multimedia designer and video maker, create hybrid design, a merger of their respective skills. They split their time between artistic experimentation and commissions, and their commercial work demonstrates the growing receptivity by upmarket brands like Giorgio Armani and Cassina, in particular, to interactive spatial design as a communication tool. Their tactics are to 'multiply the perception of space through image and of image through space [so that] static objects and spaces become alive and interactive'. 'H2O', designed for the Boffi design showroom in Paris (2004) and in Milan during the Furniture Fair (2005), is an interactive, real-time 3-D environment designed for the space. A 5 metre-long pool of water, a series of walls including a large mirror and several items of furniture are animated. Narrative elements appear: the silhouettes of a man and a woman, and new backdrops – a bathroom, swimming pool and terrace by the sea. Depending on the audience's interaction, quasi-infinity of perceptual patterns can be seen. This was teamed with 'Focus', an installation about fire – wild, sacred and domestic, in all its stages from birth to extinction – which used the floors as well as the walls as projection surfaces.

'**WARM AND COLD**', for the Paris showroom of Italian manufacturer Cassina, is a home-automation system with different lighting ambiences ranging from red (warm) to blue (cold) with a number of patterns in between, with fire, smouldering fire, ice and water that have been filmed. When someone touches the transparent, real-time 3-D heart at the centre of the room, its shape and animated texture change. As a home-automation system its innovation is a new relationship between space and image: 'The space becomes as easy to change as an image, and the image becomes more immersive.' Linking image with light ambience, as Electronic Shadow have done, provokes a new species of interfaces. The idea of a button and a remote control is replaced by more natural and poetic interfaces using elements and gestures.

THEIR TACTICS ARE TO 'MULTIPLY THE PERCEPTION OF SPACE THROUGH IMAGE AND OF IMAGE THROUGH SPACE SO THAT STATIC OBJECTS AND SPACES BECOME ALIVE AND INTERACTIVE.'
ELECTRONIC SHADOW

EXHIBITION SPACES

INTERACTIVITY IN MUSEUM AND EXHIBITION SPACES HAS LONG BEEN A BUZZWORD FOR PUSH-BUTTON DISPLAY, BUT CREATING MORE INTUITIVE AND PARTICIPATIVE EXPERIENCES IS NOW SOMETHING MANY ARE COMMITTED TO.

Interactivity in museum and exhibition spaces has long been a buzzword for push-button display, but creating more intuitive and participative experiences is now something many are committed to. Jason Bruges's interactive design for an exhibition space for the new Amnesty Human Rights Action Centre in Shoreditch, London (2005; architects Witherford Watson Mann), created with Paul Blackburn, engages visitors through simple and effective elements that are functionally defined rather than decorative. Responsive light boxes double as window shutters; light boxes showing commissioned portraits of Amnesty supporters light up when visitors approach; mobile phones are suspended from the ceiling displaying 'urgent call to action' messages. An interactive photo album displayed on the wall, 'Stand up and be counted', uses face-recognition technology to automatically add visitors to its pages. An audio map allows visitors to emotionally connect with Amnesty International stories from around the world.

AMNESTY HUMAN RIGHTS ACTION CENTRE
Permanent interactive exhibition
Jason Bruges with Paul Blackburn, 2005
(architects Witherford Watson Mann),
London, UK

MUSEUMS

Transcending the standard 'kiosk' format is something the Science Museum in London wanted to do in order to realize an engaging interactive learning environment for its new Energy Gallery (gallery design by Casson Mann[59]), which opened in 2004. Adopting an artist-led approach, the head of arts programme Hannah Redler commissioned ten installations from practitioners in media art, product and interface design, graphics and interpretative environments that would in many cases be physically demanding as well as intellectually stimulating. Kitchen Rogers Design (KRD)[60] and Robson & Jones, designers of interactive environments and objects[61] designed '**ENERGY SHUTDOWN**', a four-player tabletop digital interactive with a 3-D model cityscape, as a challenging game – restoring electricity to a city under blackout – that zaps back into life when the power returns.

ENERGY SHUTDOWN
Tabletop digital interactive
Kitchen Rogers Design (KRD) and
Robson & Jones
The Energy Gallery
(gallery design by Casson Mann),
commissioned for 'Energy: fuelling the future',
Science Museum, London
2004

'LIFELINE', an 18 metre-long interactive table, housing a virtual archive system reminiscent of one used in wartime planning, features in the new Churchill Museum (2004) designed by Casson Mann, the first museum in the UK dedicated to the life and achievements of a politician. Probably the largest interactive object within a museum to date, it can be used by up to 26 visitors at any one time who readily release new data, and dynamic imagery that sails across its surface. The work of Small Design Firm, led by David Small (born Bloomfield, Connecticut, USA, 1965), who design and construct interactive exhibits from their studio in Cambridge, Massachusetts, USA, its entire surface is spanned by projections. Over 3,000 documents written by Churchill and his contemporaries, and photographs from a century of British history, can be browsed by visitors using a new touch-based interface. Documents are arranged in chronological order and explored via touch-strips placed along the length of the table.

LIFELINE
Interactive table housing a virtual archive system
Small Design Firm
Commissioned for the Churchill Museum, London, UK (designers: Casson Mann)
2004

'Lifeline' bears traces of similarity to Small Design's earlier '**TALMUD PROJECT**', a prototype for an interactive book produced at the MIT Media Lab (1999), which explores the simultaneous display of multiple related texts. Several dials allow the reader to trace ideas from one text to another, examine translations and find text in the larger context of the entire body of work. With a combination of passages from the Koran and the Talmud in English and French translations, the software enables viewers to manipulate blocks of text into the walls, streets and windows in an imaginary city of words; it was not so surprising that an admiring critic likened it to a powerful piece of architecture.

NOBEL PEACE CENTER
Interactive installation
Nobel Peace Center, Oslo, Norway
Small Design Firm
(architect: Adjaye/Associates)
Photo: Nils Petter Dale/Nobel Peace Center

RESPONSIVEFIELDS, THE DIGITAL BEEHIVE
Tobi Schneidler with Pablo Miranda and
the Smart Studio at the Interaction Institute,
KTH Stockholm, Sweden
Commissioned by Peter Weibel for
Algorithmic revolutions exhibition, ZKM,
Karlsruhe, Germany
2004

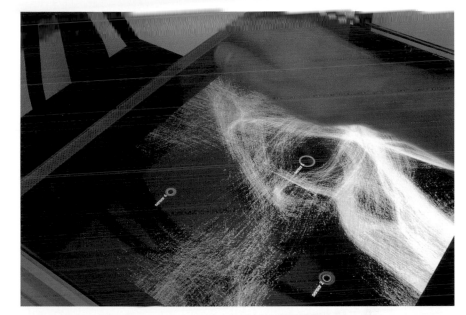

TALMUD PROJECT
Prototype for an interactive book
Small Design Firm
Produced at the MIT Media Lab, USA
Exhibited at the 1st Design Triennial,
Cooper Hewit National Design Museum,
Boston Cyber Arts Festival, 1999;
Westport Arts Center, Connecticut, 2003

CITIES OF REFUGE
(Extract from the Tractate Makkoth 10a)

These cities (of refuge) are to be made neither into small forts nor
large walled cities, but medium sized boroughs they are to be
established only in the vicinity of a water supply and where there is no
water at hand it is to be brought thither; they are to be established
only in marketing districts; they are to be established only in populous
districts, and if the population has fallen off other cities are to be brought
into the neighbourhood, and if the residents (of any one place) have
fallen off, others are brought thither, priests (cohanim), Levites and
Israelites. There should be traffic neither in arms nor in trap gear
there: these are the words of R. Nehemiah but the Sages permit.
They, however, agree that no traps may be set there nor may ropes be
left dangling about in the place so that the blood avenger may have
no occasion to come visiting there.

R. Isaac asked: What is the Scriptural authority (for all these
provisions): - The verse: and that fleeing unto one of these cities he
might live (Deuteronomy 4: 42) which means provide him with
whatever he needs so that he may (truly) live.

A Tanna taught (a baraitha): A disciple who goes into exile is joined in
exile by his master; he might live, R. Zeira remarked that this is the basis of
the dictum, "Let no one teach Mishnah ...
unworthy".

Whither are they banished? To the three cities situate
on the yonder side of the Jordan and three cities situate
in the land of Canaan, as ordained, ye shall give three
cities beyond the Jordan and three cities in the land of
Canaan; They shall be cities of refuge. Not until three
cities were selected in the land of Israel did the [first]
three cities beyond the Jordan receive fugitives, as
ordained, [and of these cities which ye shall give] six
cities for refuge shall they be unto you which means
that [they did] not [function] until all six could
simultaneously afford asylum.
And direct roads were made leading from one to the
other, as ordained, thou shalt prepare thee a way and
divide the borders of thy land into three parts. And two
[ordained] scholar-disciples were delegated to escort the
manslayer in case anyone attempted to slay him on the
way, and that they might speak to him.
R. Meir says: he may [even] plead his cause himself, as it
is ordained, and this is the word of the slayer. R. Jose B.
Judah says: to begin with, a slayer is sent in advance to
[one of] the cities of refuge, whether he had slain
him thence. Who the court

VISITOR ATTRACTIONS

VISITOR ATTRACTIONS, INCLUDING THEME PARKS, MUSEUMS AND GALLERIES, AND GARDENS, AS WELL AS HISTORIC PROPERTIES, COUNTRY PARKS AND FARMS, HAVE SOARED IN POPULARITY IN RECENT YEARS.

FLOWER OF MY SECRET
Installation: visualization
Usman Haque
Commissioned for The Public,
West Bromwich, UK
2006

THE PUBLIC
Orientation map showing position
of each exhibit
AllofUs
(architect: Alsop Architects;
interior design: Ben Kelly Design)
2004–05

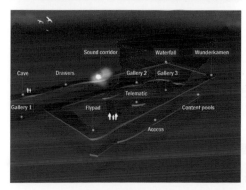

Visitor attractions, including theme parks, museums and galleries, and gardens, as well as historic properties, country parks and farms, have soared in popularity in recent years. The UK's total number stands at 6,500.[62] It is their commercial value within the tourist industry that has driven the development of themed facilities in particular, ranging from the Charles Dickens Museum to Parc Asterix in Paris. Some are developed on agricultural land owned by farmers wishing to cash in; others spring up in inner city districts as the result of community action and successful National Lottery bids for capital programme funding. As a new cultural phenomenon, they offer 'a wealth of unique experiences for international and domestic visitors alike.'[63] Sentimentalized, superficial interpretations of local history, filmic special effects can be laid on with a trowel with kitsch artistic renderings adding to mountains of themed souvenirs.

Both as a blessing and a curse, technologically mediated visitor attractions are on the rise, inevitably influenced by the ways in which new technologies are infiltrating so many aspects of our social and working lives. Few, however, strive for a truly participatory agenda exploiting their potential for new modes of play, experience and communication. The Public, in West Bromwich, England, a body championing international multi-disciplinary projects and innovations in community art, as well as creative software applications, has now created a new permanent centre due for completion in 2006.

Installations may have become easier to build nowadays, but content and curatorial and artistic intentions still need to be effectively synthesized. The focus is not on story telling, as in the conventional visitor attraction, but on visitors' own stories pieced together. This slant brings a 'live' effect to displays and allows for new interactive behaviour to emerge. When looking at an overall storyline, curators and artists alike need to consider how interactive installations can be metaphorically appropriate, yet still engaging enough to get a reaction.

The Public's inclusive agenda is carried right through to the interactive strategy for the gallery, commenced as a consultancy by Digit and more recently by Digit and AllofUs, the latter formed by five ex-Digit partners, including Nick Cristea (born Manchester, UK, 1971) and Orlando Mathias (born London, UK, 1973). Digit developed the core software, the backbone at the heart of the gallery experience, which collates and distributes content from one point to another, while AllofUs focused more on the visual visitor interfaces. AllofUs worked closely with the curatorial team

THE PUBLIC
Early concept designs for gallery spaces
with balustrade carrying input
devices
Ben Kelly Design
(architect: Alsop Architects;
visitor interfaces: AllofUs)
2004–5

to create a permanent exhibit infrastructure that independent artists including Blast Theory, Golan Levin and Zachary Lieberman, Tomas Roope with Andrew Allenson, Rolf Gehlhaar and Usman Haque, have been commissioned to make artworks for. They have also developed the digital interfaces for wayfinding and a digital representation of a visitor's data body as well as two systems essential for the visitor's entire journey through the gallery. One feature that makes the Public unique is a three-minute profiling interface for visitors at the entrance. 'Visitors are profiled so that we have some sense of their own creative direction,' says Nick Cristea. 'They are asked to leave audio samples – a shout, or a secret – visual preferences – colour, texture, movement – take photos of themselves, and leave a simple mark, like carving a tree.' All these elements are then reused by the artists in each of their artworks.

Before they leave, visitors can also use an open-ended editing tool to create new 'assets or products'. By these Cristea means images and sounds captured as people interact with all the artists' exhibits: screen grabs, generated sounds, virtual data translated in abstract patterns, elements that are reused by the artists in each of their artworks. A continuous resonant exchange occurs between artists, visitors and their respective activities. Such a process would not see the light of day without testing, and groups of visitors have been brought in to test an early prototype of the profiling process, which they found very appealing.

The whole centre is wired up, and when visitors wander around with their data bodies, they are only interacting with their own data. When they do interact with the artworks, the scope of the responsive design is very imaginative and robust. Encountering one exhibit, Usman Haque's 'FLOWER OF MY SECRET', they find a wall of drawers of various sizes positioned

THEY ARE ASKED TO LEAVE AUDIO SAMPLES – A SHOUT, OR A SECRET – VISUAL PREFERENCES – COLOUR, TEXTURE, MOVEMENT – TAKE PHOTOS OF THEMSELVES, AND LEAVE A SIMPLE MARK, LIKE CARVING A TREE.

NICK CRISTEA

at different heights, which on closer inspection are full of virtual flowerheads that teem with whispered thoughts – dreams and aspirations – visitors leave behind. Just as each secret is different, each flower has its own DNA grown from the donor's whispered audio sequence. In some of the drawers, the thoughts are audible. The design is based on reciprocity: the flowerbeds need thoughts in order to grow larger; but to hear these secrets, visitors mostly need to leave some of their own. 'The projects that we, the artists, are developing for the building are in a sense simply frameworks to encourage and elicit the interactions between people and between people and the building,' says Haque.

Tobi Schneidler is a German-born Architectural Association graduate architect who fuses digital media and physical space. He is involved in the design of a number of visitor attractions in both Europe and the Far East. Until recently he has been directing projects at the Smart Studio of the Interactive Institute, Stockholm, a multi-disciplinary research institute specializing in digital media which, through a mixture of art, technology and science, creates interdisciplinary projects generating new questions and reflections, and in 2005 set up his own consultancy, maoworks, in London. Schneidler believes that the technocratic vision should be supplanted by one that is culturally and socially driven. His project teams focus on exploring interactivity and its impact on spatial environments, evaluating this theme through physical prototyping, because the relationships between physical features, media effects and the user are too complex to explore in a physical scale model. This prototyping allows the time-based and interactive effects on users to be assessed. 'The relationship has to be modelled in time and effect,' he explains, 'rather than just as an aesthetic, scaled equivalent of the final anticipated outcome.'

META.I. HYTTAN
Tobi Schneidler and the Smart Studio
of the Interactive Institute, Sweden
Design proposal to convert Avesta Verket,
a historic steel plant, into an interactive
visitor experience
Commissioned by the Cultural Department
of Avesta City Council, Sweden
2002

'**META.L. HYTTAN**' (2002), a proposal by Schneidler and the Smart Studio for the Swedish city of Avesta to convert Avesta Verket, a historic steel plant, into an interactive visitor experience, was commissioned by the Cultural Department of Avesta City Council. It not only emerged as a scenographic design but also demonstrated how interactive technologies could be embedded in a real place and information and effects accessed in many different ways. The effects resulted from pervasive computing networks themselves hidden in the structure, and extended the space through personalized content. By giving visitors a special exploration tool, a standard flashlight, to activate them and record their journey, they could trigger interactive content as they explored the space, with the torchlight acting as a basic pointing device. The media was not delivered through typical exhibition interfaces such as touch screens or audio guides; instead, each location was individually equipped with audio and light sources, visual projections and/or kinetic actuators. These channels were then 'digitally choreographed', as Schneidler puts it, to animate each area of interest according to the personal preferences of the visitor.

The torchlight functioned as an identifier, triggering different shows adaptively, so that 'the same physical place can effectively be coloured and reshaped in response to personal interaction'. This introduced a layered set responses: 'Changing stories are told depending on the visitor's identities.' The space was divided into distinct interactive zones, each marked with a yellow ring as a hotspot. When the visitor pointed the torchlight at the hotspot, an invisible infrared signal travelled from the torchlight to the hotspot. This identified the visitor and their choice of lamp to the system in the background, which could then automatically trigger the various local media events associated with the zone. The underlying system used standard network technology, running the same protocols that operate on office networks and the global Internet.

Together with an adaptable software platform, developed by the Interactive Institute, this system became easily scalable and cost efficient. The phrase 'augmented reality' means the possibility of extending real-life environments with the help of interactive media and interfaces that link the physical space to digital information. This means that designers can overlay interactive media with physical spaces, creating new environmental entities that challenge the perception of our world. It is a potential that excites Schneidler, and to achieve it, he reckons it is necessary to see information technology not as a unit or device, but as an enabling structure that merges into the fabric of the space. Control signals, streamed media, sensors, output devices and computers are linked to that invisible system, but the effects inform a profound spatial relationship. The important achievement of the Avesta project is that the interaction experience it gives is site specific rather than media specific.

META.L. HYTTAN
Tobi Schneidler and the Smart Studio
of the Interactive Institute, Sweden
Design proposal to convert Avesta Verket,
a historic steel plant, into an interactive
visitor experience
Commissioned by the Cultural Department
of Avesta City Council, Sweden
2002

Few efforts have been made to create a physical space that lives, behaves, communicates and feels. In order to trigger a public debate about the application and implication of brain-based technology on our future society, 'ADA', the intelligent room, a multi-modal immersive interactive space, was developed for Expo 02, the Swiss national exhibition held at Neuchâtel, Switzerland, conceived by a multi-disciplinary team of up to 25 people led by psychologist Paul Vershure.[64] As an artificial organism, she had the ability to interact and communicate with visitors. In the context of the growing number of dynamically modifiable components within large, multi-purpose buildings, 'Ada', with her high level of behavioural integration and time-varying and adaptive functionality, is a rare exercise in the creation of living architecture.

Named after Lady Ada Lovelace, one of the pioneers of computer science, Ada's real-time interactions functioned continuously for ten hours a day over six months. She was programmed to balance visitor density and flow, identify, track, guide and group specific visitors, and play games with them. Visitors approached a waiting area – a 'conditioning tunnel' – where they witnessed an introduction to her components and their functions. All interaction with 'Ada' occurred in a 175 square-metre octagonal room, and in a surrounding corridor – the 'voyeur space' – visitors could observe the activities from a distance. The Brainarium, a technical display room showing the internal processing states of 'Ada', had windows so people could see into the interaction space, and on the way out they passed through the Explanatorium, which explained the key technologies behind 'Ada', and the Lab area, the operating room containing over 30 custom-built computers. 'Ada' located and identified visitors using her senses of vision, audition and touch. A 360-degree ring of 12 LCD video projectors gave her advanced visual-display capabilities so she could express her behavioural mode and internal emotional states visually to them, using the screens as a single virtual display. She could also render 3-D objects in real time, and display live video. For instance, she recorded images of 'interesting' visitors and displayed them on the visual synthesizer.

ADA: THE INTELLIGENT ROOM
Multi-modal immersive interactive space
Institute of Neuroinformatics, University
ETH, Zurich, Switzerland
Led by psychologist Paul Vershure
Installed at Expo 02, the Swiss national
exhibition, Neuchâtel, Switzerland
2002

With a 'skin' of 360 floor tiles made of pressure sensors, neon tubes and a microcontroller, 'Ada' could track her visitors, test their responsiveness to visual and sensual cues and interact with them through different games. She could also create chameleonic visual effects with the RBC-coloured neon lights in each tile. A ring of ambient lights set the overall visual emotional tone of the space, while nine gazer lights with pan, tilt and zoom capabilities made up her 'eyes'. Through two sets of microphones in the ceiling she could detect different types of sound, and their source even amid the noise of visitors. Her sound effects derived from a synthetic musical composition system called Roboser, creating a 12-voice behavioural mode-controlled soundscape. She would also 'baby talk', imitating what she heard from visitors, and with a number of moveable light fingers, point at them.

To convince even the most sceptical that 'Ada' had the properties of a natural organism, the design team made sure the operation of the space was coherent, real time, understandable to most people and offered a sufficiently rich range of possible interactions so that visitors felt the presence of 'a kind of basic unitary intelligence'. The four basic behavioural functions 'Ada' incorporated – tracking, identifying, grouping and playing with visitors – the team explains, represent a set of interconnected, interdependent, simultaneously evolving internal processes. Throughout the four-month exhibition, as 'Ada' interacted with visitors, she expressed herself in a more advanced way and grew, just like a human being would in optimal circumstances, as a result of continuing system upgrades incrementally increasing her capabilities.

EMBODIED INTERFACES FOR DANCE

KINAESTHETIC PERCEPTION IS ABOUT APPREHENDING AND NAVIGATION, ABOUT HOW OUR BODY PERCEIVES MOVEMENT THROUGH OUR HAPTIC SENSE.

Kinaesthetic perception is about apprehending and navigation, about how our body perceives movement through our haptic sense. In the field of dance, 'THE CHANGING ROOM' (2004), a dance performance incorporating live and virtual spaces, this is fully explored through the complexity of lives lived in the mediated conditions of the technological and at the edge of the real. Created by choreographer Carol Brown (born Dunedin, New Zealand, 1964) in conjunction with the architect Mette Ramsgaard Thomsen (born Copenhagen, Denmark, 1969)[65] it extends the haptic into another dimension, one in which the image or mirror of the body becomes like another dancer. Few choreographers work with embodied interfaces; their work is more about the visual than an event space of behaviours, and avoids preset interfaces. 'Screen technology has radically altered people's habits', says Ramsgaard Thomsen. 'Young people playing computer games are engaging with a mediated condition. The very ordinariness of it allows us to establish it within other cultural conditions.'

The plot of 'The Changing Room' is quite simple, involving a dresser who acts as a mediator for two characters who experience their changing room as a technological frontier. By opening wardrobes and storage units and changing their clothes, they access a series of baroque assemblages. Moving at the threshold between the virtual and the real, their gestures are tracked by a machine eye. As they do so, a series of screens embedded in the furniture of the room through which a virtual presence is rendered mirrors, extends and distorts their behaviour, allowing them to inhabit unfamiliar dimensions. At times there are pauses when the image disappears. Whether or not a digital element is an extension to a space, or a parallel presence, 'The Changing Room' demonstrates that it is something dancers and audience learn through the culture of the context.

THE CHANGING ROOM
Dance performance incorporating live
and virtual spaces
Carol Brown (choreographer) and Mette
Ramsgaard Thomsen (architect), 2003–4
Lighting design: Michael Mannion
Music: Jerome Soudan/Mimetic
Staged at the Greenwich Dance Agency,
London, UK, 2004
Photos: Mathias Eck

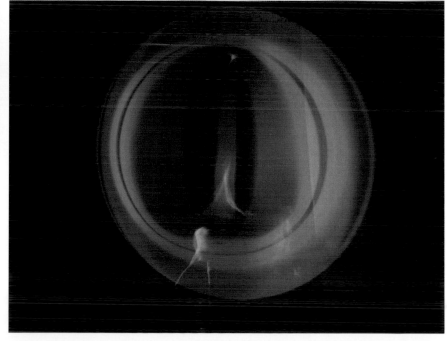

SMART DOMESTIC SPACES

SMART HOMES HAVE COME SOME WAY SINCE THE LATE 1980S, WHEN BILL GATES REVEALED THAT HIS APARTMENT IN SEATTLE HAD ART-WORKS ON THE WALLS THAT TRANSFORMED THEMSELVES AT THE TOUCHES OF BUTTONS.

REMOTEHOME: BUSY BENCH AND LONELY LAMP

Bi-locational apartment installations
Tobi Schneidler with Magnus Jonsson,
Fredrik Petersson, Carole Collett,
Erik Grönvall, Stefanie Schneidler and
Adam Somlai-Fischer, London and Berlin
Initiated by the Interactive Institute,
Stockholm, Sweden, with Central St Martins
School of Art and Design (MA Textile
Futures), London, UK 2003
Exhibited at the e-futures fair, Amsterdam,
the Netherlands, 2003; Science Museum,
London, UK; during DesignMai Berlin at the
Raumlabor, Berlin, Germany, 2003; Ludwig
Museum, Budapest, Hungary, 2004;
and touring to Moscow

Smart homes have come some way since the languid days of the late 1980s, when Microsoft founder Bill Gates revealed that his apartment in Seattle had artworks on the walls that transformed themselves at the touches of buttons. Not yet available from mass house builders except with a basic form of heat and light modulation, they are now being niche marketed to young single women in Japan. A small apartment manufactured by Brillia has a link between the flat and the owner's mobile phone, allowing her owner to turn on the air conditioning or run a hot bath remotely, so that everything is ready when she gets home from work. One extra facility allows the door entry system to transmit an image to the owner's phone of anybody who called at the flat while she was out. With her mobile, she can also check that the door is locked, and a message will be sent if the flat alarm is triggered.

Increasingly, technological customization of domestic environments will allow new, unforeseen flexibility in use. In the UK, developers David Wilson Homes with Nottingham and Leicester Universities have launched 'Project Life', a filmed experiment to find out how a typical, two parent, two children family fares for one entire week in a five-bedroom house installed with a panoply of digital devices, from self-cleaning windows and automatic shirt-ironing devices to five different remotes controlling all the house's electronic devices.

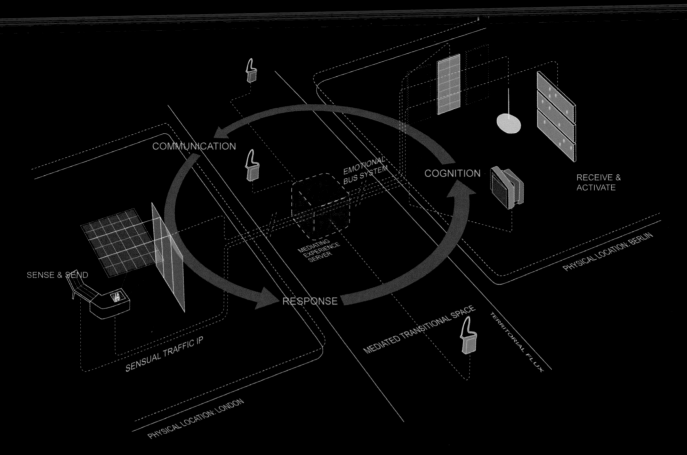

The mere fact that a firm is filming responses to its prototype intelligent home designs replete with technological gismos and convergent systems indicates a new willingness to put combined solutions to a reality test. Philips's 'Vision of the Future' project (1995), led by Stefano Marzano (art director)– a permanent exhibition, a book and a website – highlighted the multi-functionality of the future home, with products following occupants' preferences and habits.[66] The '**REMOTEHOME**' project, realized internationally by its designer Tobi Schneidler as a public installation on a number of occasions in the last few years, is quite exceptional. It is unique because it is a communication system extending the idea of home as a private and situated space to one that connects homes in two different cities. 'RemoteHome' is an apartment that exists in two countries at the same time, its floor space distributed over two cities and stitched together by digital networks. It responds to changing cultures of living and the rise of distant relationships. While communications and media technologies including mobile phones and instant messaging are already creating new scenarios of sharing friendship and intimacy over long distances, with 'RemoteHome' Schneidler asks what would happen if real time-mediated communication were to become part of our everyday environment, the spaces we inhabit, the furniture we use and the items we cherish.

REMOTEHOME: BUSY BENCH AND LONELY LAMP
Bi-locational apartment installations
Tobi Schneidler with Magnus Jonsson, Fredrik Petersson, Carole Collett,
Erik Grönvall, Stefanie Schneidler and Adam Somlai-Fischer, London and Berlin
Initiated by the Interactive Institute, Stockholm, Sweden, with Central St Martins School of Art and Design (MA Textile Futures), London, UK 2003
Exhibited at the e-futures fair, Amsterdam, the Netherlands, 2003; Science Museum, London, UK; during DesignMai Berlin at the Raumlabor, Berlin, Germany, 2003; Ludwig Museum, Budapest, Hungary, 2004;
and touring to Moscow

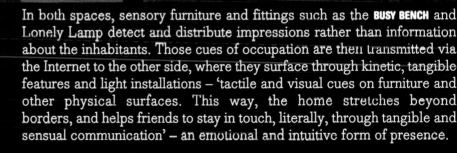

London   Berlin

In both spaces, sensory furniture and fittings such as the **BUSY BENCH** and
Lonely Lamp detect and distribute impressions rather than information
about the inhabitants. Those cues of occupation are then transmitted via
the Internet to the other side, where they surface through kinetic, tangible
features and light installations – 'tactile and visual cues on furniture and
other physical surfaces. This way, the home stretches beyond
borders, and helps friends to stay in touch, literally, through tangible and
sensual communication' – an emotional and intuitive form of presence.

Our relationship with our environments and the artefacts we handle is
increasingly changing towards the intangible: correspondence is going
digital; travel receipts are mere electronic tags; money is becoming
virtual, and the effects of mobile communication are transforming our
experience of location and geographical distance. This is proliferating
parallel worlds of experience, and triggering changes in an individual's
notion of personal context, or personal space, now meaningfully digital
as well as physical. This parallel impact also breaks down perceptions of
distance: 'RemoteHome' took that one stage further, with model apart-
ments set up by Schneidler at the Science Museum in London and the
Raumlabor in Berlin. Remote audiences could participate and interact
with each other in real time. In London an interactive lounge table was

VESTIGII TICKER CHAIR
Tobi Schneidler
Furniture for the Vestigii fashion studio,
Berlin, Germany
2005

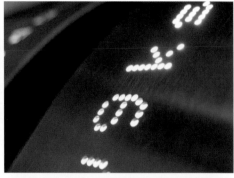

suspended from the ceiling; when someone drew on it or moved it, the surface became animated, triggering ambient music on a wall of lights in the Berlin apartment, via a sound shaft suspended over an inflatable couch. Inhabitants of this space replied with spoken messages by grabbing the sound shaft and moving it over a table. Small light sensors picked up the movement of a light beam travelling over the sensor field, relaying it to the table in London. Schneidler has seen some remote-presence projects at MIT and elsewhere, but many are 'focused on the personal device, for instance a stone that heats up and conveys presence. You don't need to show the visible technology. The simplest projects are the best,' says Schneidler. 'It's very important for me,' he adds, 'that the project is not about interactive technology or smart space per se, but about creating environments that act as mediating devices for a social statement.' Schneidler's motivation has led him to define a matrix of categories for his work, with three levels and three forms of application. The levels are personal, architectural and trans-locational, with process-based applications: concept, interactive prototype stage and real-world commissions. 'RemoteHome', uniquely of all Schneidler's work to date, embodies all three levels, stretching the conventions of physical scale, extending one environment to different locations. It is the prospect of addressing the environment as an embodied home, ephemeral, scaleable and mobile, that motivates him.

119
AFTERWORD

Since computing has become social infrastructure, as Malcolm
McCullough, author of 'Digital Ground: Architecture, Pervasive Computing
and Environmental Knowing',[67] has said, or even an aspirational second
nature, it makes sense that the technological interactivity architects,
artists and designers are forming and manipulating in their work has
evolved into a kind of medium in its own right, one that pursues and
applies scientific exploration of many kinds, social, biological, physical
and chemical, for quests of a culturally demanding nature rather than
strictly rational purposes. **RESPONSIVE ENVIRONMENTS**, by unpicking a selection
of hybrid advances made with this emerging medium, reveals some
almost magical or alchemical socially driven mediating devices – magical
in their resistance to banality.

BIOMETRICS

Biometrics is a growing technological field, used to identify people based on their biological traits, for instance DNA, real or optic fingerprints and voice. Using science to outlaw fake IDs, readers authenticate individuals based on their unique physical body demographics or behavioural characteristics: who you are is your password. Often integrated with other authentication applications and technologies, like domain access, single sign-on, smart cards, encryption, remote access and digital signatures. The downside of the ease of access and increased security it brings is loss of personal privacy.

BLUETOOTH

The wireless protocol that permits computers, phones, handhelds and peripherals to connect to each other without cables, using embedded microprocessors, for short-range communications. A radio-based technology, it is not meant to replace wireless networks but to complement them. Devices do not need to be 'looking' at each other as is the case with other wireless technologies, such as infrared, to connect. Bluetooth brings greater integration between them, more flexibility and security, and reduced power consumption, enhancing the experience of their use. See also Pervasive computing.

INTELLIGENT SKINS

Information technology and smart materials have in recent years been applied to a new set of design principles relating to the intelligent building [...]ope' (the wrapper containing the volume of space within a building) or external

fabric, enabling it to respond to external changes and internal demands. Ideally internal environmental conditions are controlled this way rather than by building services systems that consume energy. Projects such as Diller + Scofidio's Blur for the Swiss Expo'02 (see page 40) render the 'envelope' an ephemeral cloud of water vapour, and reposition the technology within 'wearables' (see wearable computing) – the plastic, electronically connected 'braincoats' worn by visitors.

INTERACTION DESIGN

Interaction design is the design of the products, services and environments made possible by information and communications technology, and of the design of people's interaction with them. A relatively new multidisciplinary field currently consolidating its methodologies, it draws on principles and methods developed in disciplines such as social psychology, linguistics and semiotics to provide structure and analytical approaches for specific contextual challenges, in anthropology and sociology to assist with the design of community-related activities, and in philosophy and psychology for contexts focusing on emotions and desires.
As technology is increasingly regarded as a medium, with computers becoming 'environments' shaping living patterns, the emphasis is moving from design products to services. This brings a dematerialization to design processes. Working largely on this plane, the practitioners featured in this book are pursuing a meaningful intangibility based on widening people's mental grasp of potential modes of physicality and emotional responses resulting from interactions with devices and processes, some based on pervasive technological means, but others relying on simple low-tech elements.

LEDS

LEDs (light-emitting diodes) are a highly versatile, relatively new lighting technology invented in 1962. Their primary role at that point was as object sensors in factories, and they only emitted infrared light. Only by the early nineties was a full range of LED colours available. They emit a very strong colour of light because unlike standard lights, they use a coloured light filter to create a specific effect. As a semiconductor within an electronic circuit, they can be dimmed or made to flash using simpler control devices than standard lamps. LEDs are also robust, potentially lasting between 30,000 and 100,000 hours.

PERVASIVE COMPUTING

Pervasive computing denotes the new generation of computing environments, with information and communication technology becoming an integrated part of environments everywhere, and potentially available for anyone, at all times. They transcend traditional user interfaces by being part of small devices and appliances, but also large-scale walls, buildings and furniture. Enabled by Bluetooth, the wireless protocol, integrated microprocessors, sensors and actuators are connected via high-speed networks and combined with visualization devices, for instance projections and large panorama displays. The phrase is often used interchangeably with ubiquitous computing. See also Ubiquitous computing.

RFID TAGS

RFID (radio frequency identity) tags were invented in 1969 and patented in 1973, but started to become commercially and technologically viable in the early years of the 21st century. Microchips, some only 1/3 of a millimetre across, they act as transponders (transmitters/responders), always listening for a radio signal sent by transceivers or RFID readers. When they receive a certain radio query (this powers them, rather than batteries), they respond by transmitting their unique ID code back to the transceiver. They are already widely in use in retail and security environments, in retail principally to manage the supply chain, including via 'smart shelves' that alert managers to the need to restock and for inventory tracking, but also in financial transactions via smart cards incorporated into mobile phones and other devices. With RFID transponders forever part of the product or documents such as passports and drivers' licences, and designed to respond when they receive a signal, anonymity and privacy could be banished. A RFID tag has been designed to go under the skin, where it can be read from 4 feet away. The growing ubiquity of RFID tags raises serious concerns about personal security. Consumers need to be notified about products with embedded RFID tags, and to be able to disable the chips and therefore any potential tracking.

RS CATALOGUE

Widely known as the 'industry bible', this is the catalogue of the UK's leading distributor RS of electronic, electrical, mechanical, health and safety products and equipment.

SENSOR AND ACTUATOR SYSTEMS

Sensors are fundamental to responsive environments. Through them, real world phenomena can be fed into a computer. While early sensors could just detect a limited amount of activity around them and pass it on to a computer for someone else to interpret, eventually they became 'smart', and as a result were put to work in manufacturing and the process industries. The technology was applied to solve real world problems. Now they are self-aware, but also in touch with other sensors, as well as actuators that let them act on what they detect. Communication, especially wireless, has become a key part of sensing systems, paying attention to what is going on, thinking about what is happening and then acting on it.

UBIQUITOUS COMPUTING

Also known as 'ubicomp', this notion, first articulated by Mark Weiser in 1988 at the Computer Science Lab at Xerox PARC (who also termed it 'calm technology'), is now often used interchangeably with the phrase 'pervasive computing'. In 1999 in his book 'When Things Start to Think' (see Further Reading), Neil Gershenfeld of MIT Media Lab coined another alternative, 'unobtrusive computing', suggesting that 'the world is the next interface', and that even money could be programmed to change value. 'Ubicomp' and its derivations refer to the imbedding or weaving of a computer into almost any form of everyday item, such as clothing, glasses, pens and coffee cups, in such a way that it is invisible and its use is seemingly natural. Early generations of computers relied on a mainframe, each shared by many people; these were replaced by personal computers,

and now in a third wave 'ubicomp' requires that computers live out in the world with people, as part of a challenging integration of human factors, computer science, engineering and social sciences. Weiser described technology as optimally 'calm' when it 'recedes into the backgrounds of our lives', but a social reading of its potential applications in the 21st century would inevitably open up searching questions amidst such apparent calm about personal privacy, as well as probe the intentionality of the interaction designers and their clients. See also Pervasive computing.

WEARABLE COMPUTING

A small computer worn on the body as reconfigurable as the familiar desktop variety and potentially always on, like an intelligent assistant or prosthetic device, observable and fully controllable by the user, yet private and unrestrictive to him or her. It can be used as communications medium, and its attentiveness to the environment gives the user increased situational awareness. Numerous applications are being designed, including the monitoring of an individual's physiology through sensors, tracking emotions and detecting depression or fear, while experimental artistic propositions include a device emitting subtle sounds in response to existing environmental conditions (a Miki Yui and Felix Hahn design), a handbag that detects air pollution (Katherine Morikawi) and other facilitators of a more malleable and intimate relationship between individuals and their surroundings. Also known as 'affective wearables'.

WIRELESS SENSING

Wireless sensor networks combine distributed sensing, computation, storage and wireless multi-hop communication. Wireless connectivity has enabled a rapid growth in mobile telephony, such as 3G, and an increasing demand for mobility in data communications. Having advanced hugely in capabilities in recent years, they are currently proving their use in a variety of scientific, military and commercial applications. They now use networks of densely deployed, inexpensive, low-power, multifunctional miniature sensor devices that can be networked together over a wireless medium to provide an overall result in sensing functionality through collaborative effort. Wireless sensing technologies will dominate the evolution of ubiquitous communications and computing in the future. See also Bluetooth.

Bender, Gretchen and Druckrey, Timothy, 'Culture on the Brink: Ideologies of Technology', Dia Center for the Arts, Discussions in Contemporary Culture, Number 9, Bay Press, Seattle, 1994

Bouman, Ole, 'RealSpace in QuickTimes: Architecture and Digitization', XIX Milan Triennale, 1996, Netherlands Architecture Institute, Rotterdam, 1996

Bourriaud, Nicolas, 'Relational Aesthetics', Les Presses du Réel, Dijon, 1998 (English translation, 2002)

Bourriaud, Nicolas, 'Post Production', Lukas & Sternberg, New York, 2005

Bullivant, Lucy (ed.), '4dspace: interactive architecture', AD/Wiley Academy, Chichester, 2005

de Kerckhove, Derrick, 'The Architecture of Intelligence', Birkhäuser, Basel/Boston/Berlin, 2001

Décosterd & Rahm, 'Architecture physiologique', Birkhäuser, Basel/Boston/Berlin, 2002

Décosterd & Rahm, 'Distortions/Architecture 2002–2005', Philippe Rahm, exhibition catalogue, FRAC Centre and Editions HYX et les auteurs, Orléans, 2005

Delft University of Technology, Faculty of Architecture, 'Gamesetandmatch, proceedings of the GSM conference', 13 December 2001 (conference director: Professor Kas Oosterhuis), Faculty of Architecture, TU-Delft, 2001

Dunne, Tony, 'Hertzian Tales: Electronic Products, Aesthetic Experience and Critical Design', Royal College of Art, 1999 and with a new introduction, The MIT Press, Cambridge, Mass, 2005/6

Electronic Shadow (Yacine Ait Kaci and Naziha Mestaoui), 'Réalités Hybrides' (English/French edition), iDEALiD, Paris, 2005

Flusser, Vilém, 'Vampyrotheusis Infernalis', Immatrix Publications, Goettingen, 1987

Fraser, John, 'An Evolutionary Architecture', Theme VII, Architectural Association, London, 1995

Gershenfeld, Neil, 'When Things Start to Think', Henry Holt and Company, New York, 1999

Graham, Stephen and Marvin, Simon, 'Telecommunications and the City: Electronic Spaces, Urban Places', Routledge, London, 1996

Guallart, Vicente and Laura Cantarella (eds), 'Media House Project: The House is the Computer, The Structure is the Network', Actar, Barcelona, 2003

Haque, Usman and Somlai-Fischer, Adam/aether architecture, 'Low Tech Sensors and Actuators', www.lowtech.propositions.org.uk

Imperiale, Alicia, 'New Flatness: Surface Tension in Digital Architecture', Birkhäuser, Basel/Boston/Berlin, 2000

Latour, Bruno and Weibel, Peter (eds.), 'Making Things Public: atmosphere of democracy', The MIT Press, Cambridge, Mass, 2005

Lee, Suzanne, 'Fashioning the Future', Thames & Hudson, London, 2005

Levin, Thomas Y., Frohne, Ursula and Weibel, Peter (eds), 'Rhetorics of Surveillance from Benthem to Big Brother', The MIT Press, Cambridge, Mass, 2002

Lozano-Hemmer, Rafael (ed.), 'Vectorial Elevation', 'Relational Architecture No.4', Conaculta Press, Mexico City, 2000 (Spanish-English bilingual edition)

Lupton, Ellen, 'Skin: Surface Substance + Design', Princeton Architectural Press, New York, 2002

Manovich, Lev, 'The Language of New Media', The MIT Press, Cambridge, Mass., 2001

McCullough, Malcolm, 'Digital Ground: Architecture, Pervasive Computing and Environmental Knowing', The MIT Press, Cambridge, Mass, 2004

Merleau-Ponty, Maurice, 'The Phenomenology of Perception', trans. Smith, Routledge and Kegan Paul, London, 1962

Moeller, Christian, 'A Time and Place: Christian Moeller, Media Architecture 1991–2003', Lars Müller Publishers, Baden, 2004

O'Mahony, Marie, Soft Machine: 'Design in the Cyborg Age' (exhibition catalogue), Stedelijk Museum, Amsterdam, 1999

Oosterhuis, Kas, 'Programmable Architecture', l'Arca Edizioni, Milan, 2002

Norman, Don, 'Emotional Design', Basic Books, New York, 2003

Pask, Gordon, 'An Approach to Cybernetics', Hutchinson & Co., London, 1961

Pask, Gordon, 'A comment, a Case History and a Plan', in Reichardt, Jasia, Rapp and Carroll (eds), 'Cybernetic Serendipity', London, 1970. Reprinted in 'Cybernetic Art and Ideas', ed. Reichardt, Jasia, Studio Vista, London, 1971, pp.76-99

Paul, Christiane, 'Digital Art', Thames & Hudson, London, 2003

Prestinenza Puglisi, Luigi, 'Hyper Architecture: Spaces in the Electronic Age', Birkhäuser, Basel/Boston/Berlin, 1999

Reichardt, Jasia (ed.), 'Cybernetic Serendipity, the Computer and the Arts', Studio International, London, 1968

Ross, Andrew, 'Strange Weather: Culture, Science and Technology in the Age of Limits', Verso, London and New York, 1991

Shedroff, Nathan, 'Experience Design 1', New Riders Publishing, Indianapolis, 2001

Spuybroeck, Lars, 'Deep Surface', exhibition catalogue, Gallery Exedra, Hilversum, 1999

(http://archittettura.supereva.com)
ARTiT (www.artit.jp)
Dorkbot (www.dorkbot.org)
Gizmodo
(http://uk.gizmodo.com/
(gadgets weblog))
GeneratorX (www.generatorx.no)
Instructables
(www.instructables.com)
Intelligent Agent
(www.intelligentagent.com)
Interactive Architecture
(www.interactivearchitecture.org)
Manovich, Lev, Info-aesthetics:
information and form, a semi-
open source book in progress,
started August 2000
(www.manovich.net)
Open Art Network (Jon Ippolito)
(www.three.org/openart)
Pixelsumo (www.pixelsumo.com)
Runme (www.runme.org)
Slashdot (www.slashdot.org)
Viralnet (www.viralnet.net)
WeMakeMoneyNotArt
(www.we-make-money-not-art.com)

Specialist magazines feature
responsive environments and
practitioners in art, architecture
and design making waves in
this field only intermittently,
and anyone wanting to get
better acquainted with their
activities needs to go online and
look at the various webzines
and blogs that have appeared in
the last year or two. The best
print magazine coverage
including cultural and social
analyses of technological
phenomena appears in:

UK:
AD (http://eu.wiley.com)
Blueprint
(www.wdis.co.uk/blueprint)
Building Design
(http://www.bdonline.co.uk)
Contemporary
(www.contemporary-
magazine.com)
Mute (www.metamute.com)

THE NETHERLANDS:
Volume (the indexes of its
predecessor Archis, are also
well worth consulting for
features and special issues;
www.archis.org)

AUSTRIA:
Springerin (www.springerin.at)

USA:
Artforum (www.artforum.com)
I.D. (www.idonline.com)
Make (www.makezine.com)
Metropolis
(www.metropolismag.com)
Technology Review (MIT,
www.technologyreview.com)
Wired (www.wired.com)

Libraries:
Besides consulting the resources
of the world's leading science
and technology libraries,
a researcher of serious intent
entering this field could consult
the Daniel Langlois Foundation
for Art, Science and Technology,
Montreal, Canada, which has
a Centre for Research +
Documentation (CR+D) with
an archive on responsive
environments; the archive at AEC
Ars Electronica Center, Linz,
Austria, one of the world's most
extensive archives of digital
media from throughout the last
twenty five years (www.aec.at);
the ZKM's Media Library in
Karlsruhe, Germany, which also
has an exhaustive collection in
this field (on1.zkm.de/zkm);
and the web-based archive run
by V2 Institute for Unstable
Media in Rotterdam, the
Netherlands, mostly focused on
its own prolific activities since
its inception in 1981
(http://framework.v2.nl/archive).

Steele, Brett (ed.), 'Corporate
Fields', AA Publications,
London, 2005

Sterling, Bruce,
'Shaping Things', The MIT
Press, Cambridge, Mass, 2005

Thackara, John, 'In the Bubble:
Designing in a Complex World',
The MIT Press, Cambridge,
Mass, 2005, (paperback), 2006

Wigginton, Michael and
Harris, 'Jude, Intelligent Skins',
Architectural Press,
London, 2002

Wilson, Steve, 'Information
Arts: Intersections of Art,
Science and Technology',
The MIT Press, Cambridge,
Mass, 2003

NOTES

All quotations in the text, unless otherwise stated, are based on interviews with the author.

1. According to From hi-tech to my tech, Richard Adams, Technology Guardian, 15 September 2005.

2. John Maeda, Fondation Cartier pour l'art contemporain, Paris/Actes Sud, Arles, exhibition catalogue, 2005, with text by Peter Weibel.

3. See Glossary.

4. Raby trained as an architect; Dunne an industrial designer. 'FLIRT' (Flexible Information and Recreation for mobile users), 1998, published by the Royal College of Art, 2000, a European Commission research project.

5. Discussed in Deep Surface, Foreword by Bart Lootsma, accompaniment to deep surface, exhibition at Gallery Exedra, Hilversum, The Netherlands. Spuybroek was born in Rotterdam in 1959; Oosterhuis, Amersfoort, 1951. In 2001 as Professor at Delft University of Technology, Faculty of Architecture, he staged Gamessetandmatch, real-time interactive architecture, 13 December 2001. See Further Research.

6. Now known as Diller, Scofidio + Renfro. Charles Renfro joined as partner in 2003.

7. Diller + Scofidio, Blur: The Making of Nothing, Harry N. Abrams, New York, 2002.

8. See Brett Steele, Corporate Fields: Office Projects by the AA Design Research Lab, AA Publications (London), 2005.

9. In Life on the Screen: Identity in the Age of the Internet, Simon & Schuster, New York, 1995.

10. In Spaces in Between, a presentation given at Computers in Theory and Art, an international symposium at Akademie Schloss Solitude, Stuttgart, 30 September – 2 October 2004.

11. One example of emotional design in Japan was the Tamagotchi (meaning loveable egg) virtual pet, created by Japanese toy manufacturer Bandai, which took the country by storm when it was launched there in 1996.

12. Its inaugural exhibition was The Museum inside the Network, NTT/ICC, Tokyo, 1996.

13. The theme of the 2005 event was Hybrid – living in paradox, coinciding with CLIMAX – the Highlight of Ars Electronica, its first Asian exhibition at the National Taiwan Museum of Fine Art.

14. Zentrum für Kunst und Medientechnologie directed by Peter Weibel.

15. Mission statement taken from the V2 website.

16. ISEA is the Inter-Society of Electronic Arts, an international organization fostering interdisciplinary academic exchange by organizations and individuals working with art, science and emerging technologies.

17. See Glossary.

18. Haque led the Open Source Architecture Workshop at Doors of Perception 8, New Delhi, 18–20 March 2005.

19. By architects Andrea Branzi and Clino Tini Castelli.

20. Thackara staged Info-eco workshops while director of the Netherlands Design Institute, Amsterdam, 1993–99; Manzini is a designer, engineer, architect, author, and Professor of Industrial Design at Milan Polytechnic; Susani is an architect, industrial designer and former Director of the Domus Academy Research Center, Milan.

21. The Experience Design Community was founded by AIGA, the American professional association for design, in 1998; Nathan Shedroff wrote Experience Design 1 in 2001, New Riders Publishing, Indianapolis, about new products, services, environments and events in this field resulting from the intersection of boundaries between interaction, information and visual and software design.

22. Emotional Design, Don Norman, Basic Books, New York, 2003, written by a cognitive scientist, although purely about static design, considered such issues as the impact of music and sound in the design of electronic equipment.

23. As Tony Dunne points out in Herzian Tales: Electronic Products, Aesthetic Experience and Critical Design, Royal College of Art, 1999, completed as a PhD thesis at the Royal College of Art, Computer Related Design Department in 1997, and published with a new introduction by MIT Press in 2006. 'Intelligent ambience' was coined by Peter Weibel in his introduction to Ars Electronica, Linz, 1994.

24. Rafael Lozano-Hemmer, Perverting Technological Correctness, Leonardo, vol.29, no.1, 1996.

25. Ito also designed the 'Dreams Room' in the Visions of Japan exhibition at the V&A, 1986, which dematerialized the city into a sensual shifting ambience.

26. www.bix.at

27. Alejandro Zaera Polo and Farshid Moussavi.

28. Architect Bruce Williams, of Koonce, Pfeffer, Bettis.

29. Launch date to be confirmed.

30. EAR is an acronym for Electronic Media Arts Research.

31. The Whitney Museum of American Art, 2002, MIT List Visual Arts Center, 2004, and La Villette, Paris, France, 2004.

32. And more recently presented at performances and exhibitions in New York, Philadelphia and Amsterdam.

33. These diagrams are used widely in anthropology and geography to describe patterns of human settlement; in biology, patterns of animal dominances and plant competitions; in chemistry, the packing of atoms into crystalline structures; in astronomy, the influence of gravity on stars and clusters; in robotics, path planning; in computer science, the solution to closest point and triangulation problems. They are even used in marketing when discussing the strategic placements of chain stores.

34. Maurice Merleau-Ponty, The Phenomenology of Perception, trans. Smith, London: Routledge and Kegan Paul, 1962.

35. Vicente Guallart is Director of the IaaC (Institute d'arquitectura avançada de Catalunya). Media House was created by a multi-disciplinary team of more than 100 people from IaaC, the Metapolis architectural studio and other bodies in Barcelona, and the Media Lab at MIT in the US.

36. With Péter Hudini and Anita Pozna.

37. Vampyrotheuthis Infernalis, Immatrix Publications, Goettingen, Germany, 1987, p.59.

38. Guest researcher at the Smart Studio, Interactive Institute, Stockholm and currently collaborating with the Media Research Centre, Department of Sociology and Communications, BUTE, Budapest, Hungary.

39. pixelACHE is the annual festival of electronic art, design and technology held at Kiasma, Museum of Contemporary Arts, Helsinki. Events are staged at other destinations including Stockholm, Bratislava, New York and Montreal. pixelACHE, a word coined by the Finnish directors of this non-profit organisation, refers to feeling an overdose of monotonous digital media content. In 2005 the theme of Dot Org Boom, the non-profit version, centred on open source communication, open content initiatives, media activist networks with a myriad of NGOs based all over the world.

40. Founded in Liverpool in 1988 as Moviola, FACT has commissioned and presented over 100 digital media artworks by artists including Mark Wallinger, Barbara Kruger, Tony Oursler and Isaac Julien.

41. Which runs a 16 month studio-based MA course focussing on emergent spatial formation, complex social organisations and new design techniques.

42. The Daniel Langlois Foundation in Montreal offers support programmes for interactive media artists.

43. Worked with Usman Haque on 'Scents of Space', 2002.

44. Collaborator with Haque on his 'Haunt' project, 2005.

45. Partner with Haque on 1000 (little tips of communication), 2004.

46. Hertzian Tales: Electronic Products, Aesthetic Experience and Critical Design, Royal College of Art, 1999. All electronic objects are a form of radio, leaking radiations into space. Urban locations in particular have a diverse and vibrant herzian culture, with mobile phone calls overlapping text messages, television broadcasts with garage door openers interfering with radio transmissions from wireless transmissions and so on (taken from the author's interview with Usman Haque, 2004).

47. Installed at the Museum of Modern Art San Francisco, USA.

48. www.d-toren.nl

49. Architect Renzo Piano. Pixelsex went live on 9 September 2005 during the Wereld van Witte de Witt Festival. Based on Roth's scientific research on cellular automata, a pixel wall conceived as a large-scale urban event turned the façade into a matrix of amoebae.

50. Founded in 1997 by Chris Salter, director, composer and interactive design/Information architect, mathematician Sha Xin Wei and performance artists Laura Farabough.

51. See Glossary.

52. At the 2001 Ars Electronica Festival.

53. Klein Dytham architecture (Mark Dytham, born Northamptonshire, UK, 1964 and Astrid Klein, born Varese, Italy, 1962)

54. Born Turin, Italy, 1968. Ciccio means 'Curiously inflated computer controlled interactive object'.

55. Building as interface, or, what architects can learn from interaction designers, Stefano Mirti and Walter Aprile, in Lucy Bullivant (guest editor), 4dspace: Interactive Architecture, AD/Wiley Academy, 2005. Walter Aprile was born in 1971 in Parma, Italy.

56. Born London, UK, 1974. Dominic Robson was born London, 1966. See also page 100.

57. Originally planned for the Salone del Mobile/Milan Furniture Fair.

58. See Glossary.

59. Exhibition, museum and interior designers Dinah Casson (born London, 1946) and Roger Mann (London, 1959)

60. KRD founding directors Shona Kitchen and Ab Rogers now work independently under their own names.

61. Robson & Jones are Crispin Jones and sound artist Dominic Robson. They develop interactive environments and objects for public spaces.

62. According to the British Government's Department for Culture, Media and Sport website, 2005.

63. Ibid.

64. Based at the Institute of Neuroinformatics, ETH, Zurich, Switzerland.

65. Mette Ramsgaard Thomsen runs escape (founded 2003) with computer scientist Jesper Mortensen, which designs site specific interfaces and digital environments for architecture, design and games. She is Head of the Centre for Interactive Technologies and Architecture (CITA) at the Royal Academy of Fine Arts, Copenhagen, and a research fellow at Brighton University, UK.

66. Vision of the Future, V+K, 1995, and in 1999, Home of the near future (Philips Design).

67. MIT Press, 2004.

INDEX